SAMPAN GIRL SMILES

舢板女孩的微笑

国家文物局水下文化遗产保护中心
宝德中国古船研究所 编

尤泽峰　姜波　编著
大卫·威利·沃特斯　摄影
黄临风　周昳恒　翻译

Editor: Zefeng YOU　Bo JIANG
Photographer: David Willie Waters
Translator: Linfeng HUANG　Yiheng ZHOU

上海古籍出版社

编辑委员会

主　　任：宋建忠

副主任：姜　波　尤飞君

委　　员（以姓氏笔画为序）：
尤泽峰　何国卫　林　歆　周昳恒　袁晓春
袁雁悦　黄临风　黄　艳　常方舟　史蒂文·戴维斯

核　　校：史蒂文·戴维斯　何国卫

Compilation Committee

Director: Jianzhong SONG
Deputy Director: Bo JIANG　Feijun YOU

Committee Members:　Zefeng YOU　Guowei HE
　Xin LIN　Yiheng ZHOU
　Xiaochun YUAN　Yanyue YUAN
　Linfeng HUANG　Yan HUANG
　Fangzhou CHANG　Stephen Davis

Proofread:　Stephen Davis　Guowei HE

序 言

2011年初,在大卫·威利·沃特斯(David Willie Waters)100岁生日之际,一位研究中国海洋商船的船舶设计师拜访了他,以了解更多他在这个领域的开拓性研究。这位访客事后回忆说:"在第一次会面时,沃特斯就显得十分激动。"他解释说,这样的情绪化反应,不仅是由于涌起的关于中国的遥远回忆,同时还因为,终于有一位船舶设计师对他的早期研究充满热情。

20世纪30年代,沃特斯在中国和日本担任了两期英国皇家海军初级官员。期间,他对中国船进行了详细研究。他拍摄了数百张关于传统船只和造船工艺的照片,编制了四卷期刊(并添加彩图以丰富文本),并委托中国造船师制作了大量等比例缩小的中国舟船模型。他陆续将其中的七艘模型捐赠给了位于格林威治的英国国家海事博物馆,随后成为了该博物馆的高级职员,最终升任为副馆长,直到1976年退休。目前,部分精美舟船模型正在我馆一处常设展览中展出。沃特斯的捐赠品为这个开创性的展览以及配套书籍奠定了基础。

沃特斯的舟船作品和他的基础研究,填补了中国海洋史与传统船舶研究的空白。因此,自己的成果在多年以后被研究人员咨询,并受到中国大众的喜爱,这无疑让沃特斯非常欣喜。在目睹这本书籍实现出版的同时,我个人也分享着这份喜悦。英国国家海事博物馆是英国皇家格林威治博物馆的四个组成部分之一,这里储存着不可思议的财富,包括文物、艺术品和档案。到目前为止,沃特斯的作品还在众多的珍宝中默默无闻。因此,我们博物馆欢迎尤泽峰先生和宝德中国古船研究所作为先行者,以大卫·威利·沃特斯的卓越努力与学术成果为基础,开展一系列的相关项目。

凯文·菲斯特博士
皇家艺术协会会员
英国皇家格林威治博物馆馆长
2017年4月

Preface

In early 2011, with David Willie Waters about to celebrate his 100th birthday, a naval architect researching Chinese sea-going trading junks visited Waters at his home to learn more about his pioneering research in this field. The visitor later recalled that Waters "was visibly emotional at our first meeting. He explained that his sentimental reaction was due in part to the flood of distant memories of his time in China, but also to the fact that finally a naval architect had been sufficiently enthused by his early work."[1]

Waters had served two terms in China and Japan in the 1930s as a Royal Navy junior officer, during which time he undertook a detailed study of Chinese junks; taking hundreds of photos of traditional craft and boat building, compiling four volumes of journals (with water-colours augmenting the narrative text), and commissioning a Chinese boat builder to construct numerous scale-models of Chinese junks. He subsequently donated seven of these to the National Maritime Museum in Greenwich and later joined the Museum's senior staff, eventually rising to be deputy director before retiring in 1976. Several of these splendid models are currently displayed in one of our permanent exhibitions. The Waters collections form the basis for this ground-breaking exhibition and companion book.

The Waters collections and his underpinning research fill major gaps in Chinese maritime history and traditional boat research. Waters would thus no doubt have been delighted that, after so many years, his work is again being consulted by researchers and enjoyed by the general public in China. I share his joy in seeing this project realised. The National Maritime Museum, one of the four Royal Museums Greenwich component sites, is the repository for incredible riches-objects, artworks and archive collections. Until now, amidst all these treasures, the Waters collection has gone largely unnoticed. The Museum thus welcomes the initiative taken by Mr. Zefeng You and the Institute of Ancient Chinese Ships to develop several projects based on David Willie Waters' remarkable efforts and scholarship.

Dr. Kevin Fewster AM FRSA
Director, Royal Museums Greenwich
April, 2017

---

[1] Michael Trimming, *The Mariner's Mirror*, Vol97:3, August 2011, p.119.

前 言

"小女孩拿起斑驳的橹,有模有样地划起水来,就像她父母平日里做的那样。望着小女孩天真活泼的模样,舢舨上的父母相视而笑,笑声飘散在风中海里,引得鸟儿跟着欢声歌唱。"

记录下可爱舢板女孩的摄影师是一位西方古船研究者——英国人大卫·威利·沃特斯(David Willie Waters)。他于20世纪30年代,先后数次跟随英国海军来到亚洲,到达中国沿海一带。期间,他凭着自己的专业素养与独到视角,拍摄了当时停泊在沿海港口里各式各样的木帆船以及生活、劳作于此的芸芸众生,包括舢舨上的这位可爱女孩。

正因为沃特斯先生的有心记录,才有了我与小女孩的"初次相遇"。记得那是2016年3月,当时刚在格林威治天文台参加完国际海事博物馆协会理事会,我在英国皇家格林威治博物馆馆长凯文·菲斯特博士(Dr.Kevin Fewster)的陪同下,于英国国家海事博物馆图书馆首次见到了这批照片资料,四本厚厚的相册,两本斑驳的日记,有些脱落的皮质封面,愈加散发出厚重的历史感。虽然研究中国航海与舟船文化已经多年,但是第一次见到如此完整、成批地讲述中国舟船的照片,兴奋之情不禁溢于言表。

中国舟船文化历史悠久,传统造船工艺精湛无比,但是世人对于传统舟船的研究,却远不及舟船历史本身丰富多彩。而沃特斯先生拍摄的这批照片,真实记录了20世纪30年代中国沿海乃至东南亚的传统舟船、造船工艺及海港风情,这无疑为"海上丝绸之路"与传统造船史等方面的研究提供了极其珍贵的新材料。

沃特斯先生的足迹成了我们编排此书的灵感,由山东威海港开始,沿着海岸一路南下,以港口为经、舟船为纬,先境内再境外,逐港、逐船介绍,力求将沿海古港中的片片帆影,串成一条鲜活的"海上丝绸之路",以精彩再现中国传统舟船的风姿绰影。

让我们再次将目光聚焦到 20 世纪 30 年代。被拍下这张照片后，小女孩好奇地目送陌生的外国摄影师离开，她并不知道自己的笑容将从此定格在历史长河中，并为后世留下珍贵的资料与无尽的遐想。她只是寻着父母指去的方向，不紧不慢地划着舢板，慢慢驶向前方的大船。

小小的舢板轻轻荡开一圈又一圈的涟漪，仿佛是缓缓拉开的幕布，即将登场的便是关于这批舟船的迷人故事。

尤泽峰

2017 年 5 月

Foreword

"The little girl picked up the mottled oar, rowing just like how her parents did everyday. The girl's innocence and liveliness made her parents standing on the sampan laugh satisfied. Their laughter drifted away in wind and in sea, with birds singing at the top of their voice."

The photographer who recorded the cute girl on the sampan was David Willie Waters from the United Kingdom. He came to Asia with the British naval forces several times in the 1930s, reaching as far as coastal ports in China. During his stay, Mr. Waters not only took the picture of the girl with a big smile on the sampan, but also recorded ports of different styles in China's coastal areas in the early 1930s, various wooden sailing boats and lovely fisherfolk living on the bank and on boats.

It was because of Mr. Waters's photos that I had the "first encounter" with that little girl. I remembered it was in March 2016, after participating in the executive committee meetings of the International Council of Maritime Museums at the Royal Observatory in Greenwich. Accompanied by the Director of Royal Museums Greenwich, Dr. Kevin Fewster, I read this series of materials at the National Maritime Museum's library: four thick albums and two spotted diaries. The leathery cover was abraded, but its historical depth made me excited. Although I had studied Chinese maritime and traditional vessels for years, I still could not help but express my excitement on sight of such a complete batch of photographs narrating China's ports and vessels.

The history of Chinese vessels is rich and long, with advanced techniques of traditional shipbuilding. However, research on Chinese traditional vessels is far less rich than its history. Photos shot by Mr. Waters have preserved a true record of the traditional ships, shipbuilding techniques and port styles of Chinese and South-East Asian coastal areas in the 1930s and thus can have served as precious materials for studies of "Maritime Silk Road" and traditional shipbuilding history.

Through Mr. Waters's lens, the girl on the sampan is part of a most treasurable reference for studying Chinese traditional wooden sailing boats and the social customs of coastal ports. It has also filled the gap in modern Chinese maritime history. This might be the possible "surprise" left by Mr. Waters.

Let's refocus our minds on the 1930s. After being captured in this photo, the little girl gazed after the departing foreign photographer. She did not know that her smile would be preserved in the photo, leaving behind the precious historic material and a source of endless imagination for later generations. She was paddling the sampan, not in a hurry, following the direction of her parents' calling and slowly heading for the big boat.

The water rippled for a long while with the progress of the sampan. It was like raising the curtain gradually before the story of these ancient vessels appeared on stage.

Zefeng YOU
May, 2017

目录 | CONTENTS

序言 / 1
Preface

前言 / 1
Foreword

山东 / 1
Shandong

威海港 / 2
Weihai Port

北直隶商船 / 5
Beizhili (Pechili) Trading Junk

安东商船 / 8
Andong (Antung) Trading Junk

烟台港 / 12
Yantai Port

芝罘船 / 15
Zhifu (Chefoo) Junk

沙船舵 / 16
Sand Junk (Sha Chuan) Rudder

青岛港 / 18
Qingdao (Tsingtau) Port

青岛渔船 / 20
Qingdao (Tsingtau) Fishing Junk

山东商船 / 23
Shandong Trading Junk

披水板 / 26
Leeboard

上海 / 29
Shanghai

上海港 / 30
Shanghai Port

舢板 / 32
Sampan

橹 / 35
Yuloh (Sculling Oar)

崇明运棉船 / 37
Chongming Cotton Junk

浙江 / 39
Zhejiang

杭州湾商船 / 41
Hangzhou Bay Trading Junk

船艏/船艉图案 / 45
Patterns on Bow and Stern

宁波港 / 46
Ningbo Port

绿眉毛船(舟山船) / 48
Green Eyebrow (Zhoushan) Junk

船帆 / 52
Sail

福建 / 55
Fujian

泉州港 / 57
Quanzhou Port

泉州商船 / 58
Quanzhou Trading Junk

厦门港 / 60
Xiamen (Amoy) Port

厦门商船 / 62
Xiamen (Amoy) Trading Junk

厦门渔船 / 64
Xiamen (Amoy) Fishing Junk

厦门盐船 / 66
Xiamen (Amoy) Salt Junk

船眼 / 69
Ship's Eye (Oculus)

花屁股船 / 70
Flowery Stern (Hua Pi Gu) Junk

福船舵 / 73
Stern Rudder

福船 / 74
Pole Junk

福建三都澳船 / 82
Fujian Sandu Bay Trading Junk

海神妈祖 / 85
Sea Goddess *Mazu*

广东 / 87
Guangdong

潮州港 / 89
Chaozhou Port

汕头港 / 91
Shantou (Swatow) Port

汕头渔船 / 93
Shantou (Swatow) Fishing Junk

汕头商船 / 94
Shantou (Swatow) Trading Junk

广州港 / 96
Guangzhou (Canton) Port

广东盐船 / 99
Guangdong Salt Junk

开孔舵 / 105
Fenestrated Rudder

阳江港 / 109
Yangjiang (Yeung Kong) Port

七艕 / 110
Seven Pang (Qi Pang)

海南商船 / 115
Hainan Trading Junk

香港 / 119
Hong Kong

香港港 / 121
Hong Kong Port

筲箕湾 / 124
Shau Kei Wan

香港仔 / 127
Aberdeen

吐露港 / 131
Tolo Harbour

九龙湾渔船 / 139
Kowloon Bay Fishing Junk

香港渔船 / 143
Hong Kong Fishing Junk

澳门 / 145
Macau

澳门港 / 146
Macau Port

罗刹船 / 148
Lorcha Junk

澳门渔船 / 153
Macau Fishing Junk

水密隔舱 / 157
Watertight Bulkhead

东南亚所见中国船 / 159
Chinese ships seen in South-East Asia

越南北圻 / 161
Tonkin Vietnam

新加坡港 / 162
Singapore Port

参考文献 / 168
References

后记 / 170
Postscript

山 东
Shandong

威海港 | Weihai Port
烟台港 | Yantai Port
青岛港 | Qingdao (Tsingtau) Port

"在我们北方,新船下水仪式可热闹了,船在下水时在船头挂上两块红布,叫作'挂红子'。我是船东,要烧香、叩头,还要宰杀大公鸡,用鸡血滴在船前的迎风板上。然后燃放鞭炮,宴请前来祝贺的亲朋好友、捻匠及木匠等人,我们当地叫'请老师'。"

——山东船东

"In the north region, the launching ceremony can be more than lively—usually we hang two red cloths in the bow for a newly launching junk , which we called 'Red Hung'. I am the ship owner, so I need to burn incense, kowtow, and slaughter a rooster, with chicken blood dripping on the bow, then set off firecrackers, to banquet friends and family, caulking men and carpenters who came to congratulate us—these we called 'please masters'."

—Ship owner from Shandong

威海港

威海港为不冻良港，位于今山东半岛东北端威海市，濒临黄海，东面有刘公岛作为屏障，西连烟台、蓬莱，北隔渤海海峡，与辽东半岛旅顺口成犄角之势。威海港是军港，刘公岛曾为北洋水师的核心基地，也是近代山东对外开放的重要通商口岸。1918年该港修建栈桥式"德胜"码头，1930年和记洋行兴建"和记"码头。从威海港出发，往北可与天津、沈阳直接通航，往南可与浙江、福建等地进行贸易往来。

威海港 | Weihai Port

Weihai Port

Weihai Port is an ice-free harbour which sits on Weihai City in the northeast of Shandong Peninsula and faces the Yellow Sea. With Yantai and Penglai to the west and Liugong Island sheltered in the east, the port points to the Lüshunkou Port in the Liaoning Peninsula across the Bohai Strait. Weihai Port was a naval harbour, as the Liugong Island was once the core base for the Beiyang Fleet. In addition, it was also one of Shandong's most important commercial ports in modern times. Port developments included the pile-supported Desheng Wharf, built in 1918. In 1930, a second wharf, the Heji Wharf, was built by International Export Company Kiangsu Limited. The Weihai Port owned a shipping route which reached Tianjin and Shenyang in the north, and traded with Zhejiang and Fujian in the south.

北直隶商船-1
Beizhili (Pechili) Trading Junk-1

北直隶商船

北直隶商船是指往返于营口、上海、江西和浙江各港的北方船。顺风时，该船从营口驶抵上海一般只需 5 个昼夜。北直隶商船长 42~54 米，宽 6~9 米，载重量约为 200~300 吨，每船船员 22~30 人。船身少有装饰，每年涂一次起防护作用的桐油。有 5 根桅杆，布置特别。前桅立于靠左侧舷墙，两根主桅在船中纵成为一条直线，后桅立于船艉，与舵杆成一条直线，舵杆左侧再立一根更小的尾桅，一般只在调戗或微风行驶时采用。船帆的两缘笔直，帆身高而窄，前桅和主桅之间常见一片索帆，亦有比较罕见的顶帆。这种布置既能提供足够的帆面积，又能分片使用方便吊戗和偏航。船员在从船艉伸出的一个长 3~4 米的操纵台上驾驶艉帆，住所位于船艉的甲板室。

Beizhili (Pechili) Trading Junk

Beizhili trading junk operated the coastal trade between Yingkou in Liaoning, and ports in Shanghai, Jiangxi and Zhejiang. It took only five days from Yingkou to Shanghai off the wind. A typical Beizhili trading junk measured 42~54 metres in length and 6~9 metres in beam, with a load capacity of 200~300 tons, and could accommodate 20~30 crewmembers. Its hull was rarely decorated but left plain, with Tung oil applied annually for protection. The rigs had five masts with a special arrangement. The first, or bow mast was offset against the port bulwark. The two principal masts—the foremast and mainmast— were on the centreline. In the aftmost part of the main hull, a mizzenmast was set in a straight line with rubberstock. Slightly forward of it, offset on the port bulwark and canted outwards, was a smaller quartermast used while adjusting direction or sailing under gentle breeze. The sails were tall and narrow, with straight luffs and leeches. Between the foremast and the mainmast there was often a staysail, and the mainmast could carry a topsail, something not commonly seen in other junk types. By adjusting each element of the complex rig independently, balance and manoeuvrability were enhanced. The mizzen sheets were taken out to a light, framework quarter gallery extending some 3~4 metres from the top of the transom. The accommodation was situated below the poop and quarterdeck.

北直隶商船-2~4
Beizhili (Pechili) Trading Junk-2

安东商船

安东商船是指往返于安东（今丹东）和上海之间的北方船，途中有时会停靠于大连、芝罘和威海卫。该船行驶缓慢，顺风时单程也需要六七天。这种船大小不等，小的载重 50 吨，大的载重可达 250 吨。其结构特征为：船头平削成箱型，干舷较低，船艉高翘，从头至尾形成高曲度的弧线；无舷墙，航行时船舯甲板几乎完全浸泡在海水中，船员由船甲板中纵处往来于船艏和船艉；通常是四桅，前桅前倾超过船头，主桅立于船舯，桅帽上装有滑轮，中间有升降绳穿过，较小的两根后桅立于船艉甲板的两侧。船老大在船艉板至甲板屋后侧之间的井型座舱驾驶船只。除了船身和桅杆涂黑后罩一层清漆，船艏和船翼板贴红色神纸外，通常无其他装饰。

Andong (Antung) Trading Junk

The Andong trading junk was a northern junk type that traded between Andong (now Dandong) and Shanghai. It would sometimes stop en route at Dalian, Zhifu (now Yantai) and Weihaiwei, a slower route than sailing direct and taking six or seven days even though the passage was off the wind. These boats varied in size from 50 tons up to 250 tons, and had a peculiar structure with the following characteristics: a square bluff bow, lower amidships and above a raised stern, forming a distinctive curvature when observed from abeam. There were no bulwarks, so the waist deck was almost awash while sailing laden. The crew moved between the bow and the stern via the deck amidships over the cargo holds. The Andong trading junk had four masts, though often only one of the two mizzens was rigged at any one time. The foremast in the eyes of the junk canted forward over the bow. The mainmast stood amidships, its truck with sheaves for the halyards and lifts. In the stern two smaller aftermasts were set on each quarter. The captain steered the junk in a well-shaped cabin between stern and deckhouse. The hull and masts were painted black with a thin layer of varnish; the bow and wings were pasted with red gods. There was no other decoration.

安东商船-1 | Andong (Antung) Trading Junk-1

安东商船-2、3 | Andong (Antung) Trading Junk-2、3

烟台港

烟台港位于山东半岛芝罘湾北侧,扼守南北洋航线中段,港阔水深,常年不冻,冬季亦可通航。1861年8月,烟台港被辟为开放口岸,同时设立了东海关。清同治年间,东海关建造了海关码头与崆峒岛灯塔。1901~1921年,又先后建成东、西公共码头和东、西防波堤。20世纪30年代末,港口年吞吐量已达68万吨。烟台港有着广阔的经济腹地,是山东及邻近的山西、陕西、河南、河北诸省的货物中转站,也是中国北方与日本、俄国、朝鲜贸易的中心。

Yantai Port

Yantai Port is located in the north of Zhifu Bay on the Shandong Peninsula and in the middle of the north-south sea route. It has a wide harbour with deep water and is ice-free all year round, which makes the port navigable during winter time. In August of 1861, the port was opened officially as the earliest international trading port; meanwhile the Zhifu Customs was established. During the Tongzhi Reign of the Qing Dynasty, the Zhifu Customs constructed the Customs Wharf and a lighthouse on Kongtong Island. Between 1901 and 1921, the East and West Public Wharf, as well as the East and West Bulwark were built successively. By the end of the 1930s, the handling capacity of the port had reached 680,000 tons. Yantai had a vast economic hinterland and was a cargo transit point for Shandong and its neighbouring provinces including Shanxi, Shaanxi, Henan and Hebei, as well as a centre of trade between northern China and Japan, Russia, and Korea.

烟台港 | Yantai Port

芝罘船-1、2 | Zhifu (Chefoo) Junk-1、2

芝罘船

芝罘船又称烟台船，有商船和渔船之分。直到1923年，这种船在海参崴地区依然还很常见。芝罘商船主要航行于北直隶湾（今渤海湾）各港口之间，结构与安东船非常相似，四桅，长21~24米，宽6米。芝罘渔船作业于寒冷地区，长9~11米，宽3米。该船在通往船员住舱的舱口常施加雕刻等装饰。船体用松木建造，结构牢固，按常规分成几个水密隔舱，用于储存捕获的鱼虾。这种船的主要特点是：甲板平铺到船舷，船艏和船艉较高，船舯干舷很低，中间形成曲度较大的弧形；船艉的舷墙高出主甲板约2.4米，形成为舵工遮风挡浪的防护体；船上竖2根桅杆，前桅前倾，立于船眼连线处，主桅立于船舯，挂北方方形帆，两帆都悬挂于桅杆的左侧。

Zhifu (Chefoo) Junk

The Zhifu junk, whether for trading or fishing purposes, was also called the Yantai junk. This type of vessel was still sailing to the Vladivostok area until 1923. However, its main sailing area was the ports in Beizhili Gulf (now Bohai Gulf), and its structure was very similar to the Andong junk. It was 4-masted, 21~24 metres long, and 6 metres in beam. The Chefoo fishing junk faced being frozen because it mainly operated in waters where sea ice was common. It measured 9~11 metres in length and 3 metres in beam. The hatches leading to the crew accommodation often had carved decoration. The solidly built hull was usually made of soft wood such as pine, and internally was separated into several watertight compartments for storing fishes. The ship's main features were a foredeck rising to the bow, and a raised bow and stern with lower freeboard amidships, giving the hull a pronounced sheer. The stern bulwarks were raised about 2.4 metres above the main deck, protecting the helmsmen against wind and waves. The fishing junk had two masts: the foremast canted forward in the eyes of the ship with the mainmast amidships. Both had northern-type square sails, both rigged on the left side of the mast.

沙船舵

沙船舵是升降舵，沙船尾部假尾上搭有舵楼，为升降舵的上下提供了空间。舵体分舵杆和舵叶两部分，明代沙船舵的舵杆一般取材榆木、榔木和楮木，清代多用楸木，舵叶常用杉木制成。沙船一般使用不平衡舵，不少舵叶上部靠近舵杆处有开口，主要供悬吊用。舵叶在高度方向的尺寸通常称为"展"，宽度方向的尺寸通常称为"舷"，沙船舵叶的展舷比较小，相对来说转舵比较费力气。

Sand Junk (Sha Chuan) Rudder

A sand junk was a typical type of junk that employed a hoistable rudder. The raised poop at the stern provided enough space for lifting the deep rudder clear of the water. In the Ming Dynasty, rudder stocks were generally made from elm or chestnut, whereas in the Qing Dynasty green catalpa was more commonly used. The rudder blade was made of fir. The sand junk commonly used an unbalanced rudder, with openings at the top of rudder blade near the stock for the ropes by which the rudder was suspended. The height unit of the rudder blade was usually called "Zhan", while width dimensions were usually called "Xian", and the rudder size was kept to a proportion of approximately 1.0, which required more effort to steer.

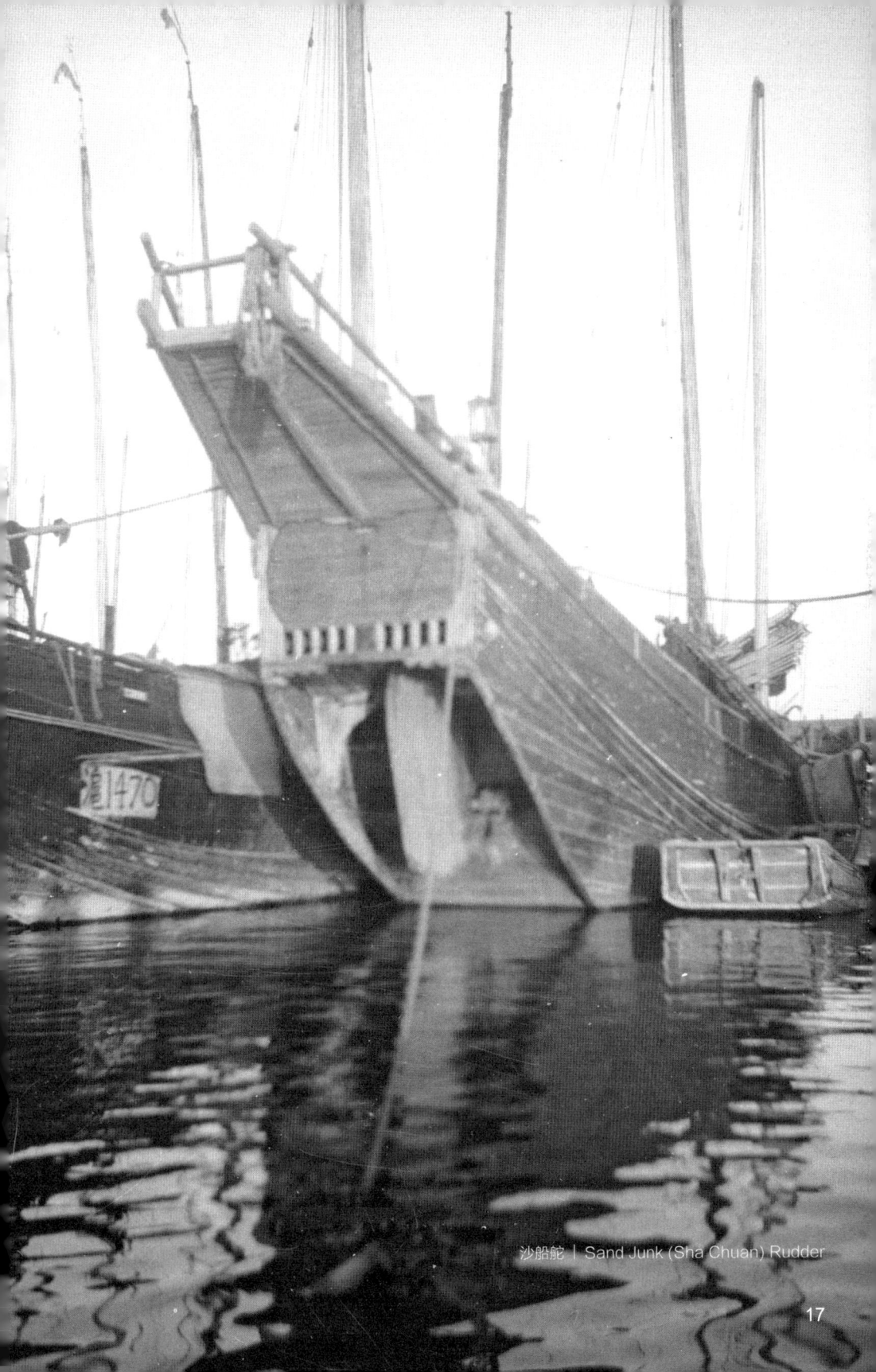

沙船舵 | Sand Junk (Sha Chuan) Rudder

青岛港

青岛港位于山东半岛东南部的胶州湾,既是商港,也是军港。因其优越的自然条件和地理位置,历来是中国北方一带重要的贸易港口,并与朝鲜、日本有贸易通道。1930年代,青岛港归国民党政府统治,设青岛市港务局统一管理经营,基本保持德占时期原貌,并加强了码头运输业务。这一时期,远洋航线可至日本、欧美等国,沿海航线北可至沈阳,南可达上海、宁波、福州、香港等地。

Qingdao (Tsingtau) Port

Qingdao Port was located in Jiaozhou Bay in the southeast of the Shandong Peninsula, serving both as a harbour and a military port. Due to its excellent natural conditions and geographical location, it had always been important to northern area maritime trade, whilst also serving as an important link between Korea and Japan. In 1930, during the Kuomintang government period it was controlled under unified regulations set by the Qingdao Port authorities. Its port's original appearance from its period of German occupation was well maintained and its maritime transportation business strengthened. During this period, deep sea routes extended to Japan, Europe and across the Pacific to the Americas, while coastal routes reached as far north as Shenyang (Mukden), and in the south to Shanghai, Ningbo, Fuzhou, Hong Kong, etc.

青岛港-1,2 | Qingdao (Tsingtau) Port-1,2

青岛渔船

青岛渔船主要作业在青岛近海的灵山岛、崂山湾、潮连岛等海域的渔场。这种船通常用松木等软木制造，结构牢固，船体被分成几个隔舱用于存放捕获的鱼虾。船为平底，吃水较浅。甲板为平铺式，船艏平削成箱形，船舯干舷很低，船艉高翘，中间形成曲度很大的弧形。船艉两侧翼板为开放式，两翼板用一根横梁连接，横梁和甲板的正中有一铰辘，用于起吊装在舵井里的舵，设有井型座舱供船员驾驶。船上竖两桅，前桅前倾，主桅立于船舯，悬挂北方的矩形帆。

青岛渔船 | Qingdao (Tsingtau) Fishing Junk

Qingdao (Tsingtau) Fishing Junk

The Qingdao fishing junk operated mainly on Lingshan Island, Laoshan Bay, Chaolian Island and other neighbouring offshore fisheries. This type of junk was usually made of softwoods, such as pine. It had solid structure with the hull divided into several compartments to store fish and prawns. It had a flat bottom, a shallow draft, planked deck and a square-cut bow. The low freeboard amidships and the raised stern gave the junk a pronounced sheer. The raised stern was open, with wing panels each side, across the tips of which was a windlass for hoisting the rudder. The crew steered in a well-shaped cabin. There were two masts, the fore canted forward and the main amidships, both with northern-type square sails.

山东商船-1 | Shandong Trading Junk-1

山东商船

山东商船一般往返于山东各港，出入烟台、莱州等重要港口。石岛湾商船就是其中的一种，长24~30米，宽3~4.5米，载重70~250吨。这种船通常为四桅，前桅向前倾斜，主桅立于船舯。船头呈方形，平铺甲板，结构牢固，船头舷墙上弯曲弧度较大。船艄两侧翼板呈开放式，外倾角度很大；船艉呈箱形，并伸出一个约2米的平台。船艏装饰艳丽，引人注目，四方形的船艏板被涂红，中央有一白圈，上用黑漆写一个"府"字，船艏两侧被漆成绿色，有船眼，船体大部分罩深红光漆。

Shandong Trading Junk

Shandong trading junks traded between the ports in Shandong Province such as Chefoo and Laizhou. The Shidao Bay trading junk was an example of this kind, with a length of 24~30 metres, a beam of 3~4.5 metres, and capable of carrying 70~250 tons. Such vessels typically had four masts: foremast tilted forward, and the mainmast stood amidships. They were solidly built with a square bow, planked deck, and with forward bulwarks curving up strongly. Both the bow wings leaned well outward. The box-shaped stern created a platform about 2 metres long. The junk had appealing, bright and dramatic bow decoration with the square bow plate painted red and a white circle in the centre, inside of which was the Chinese character "Fu" (府) in black. Both sides of the bow were coloured in green. In addition to this, there was an oculus, or eye. The rest of the hull was painted deep red.

山东商船-2 | Shandong Trading Junk-2

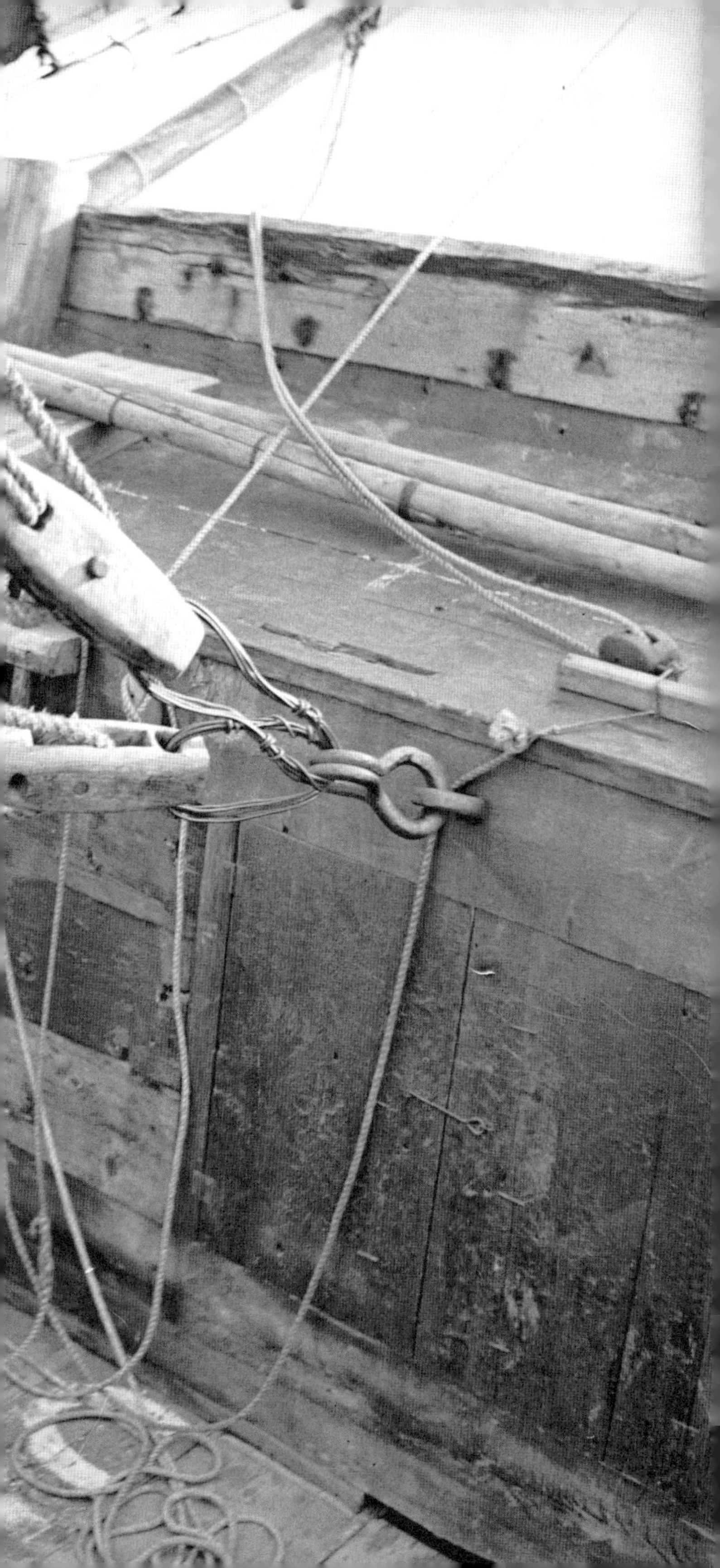

披水板

披水板是木帆船驶风的辅助工具，明代称腰舵，清代称橇头。披水板一般是一块长方形的硬杂木，其材质通常为桐木、栗木和椐木。尺寸上窄下略宽，长度一般等于船宽，厚度则根据长度变化。平时悬挂在船中部两舷侧各一块，一般用拉索升降。驶偏风时将下风舷的一块提放到水中，以减小或阻止船体横移。当沙船遇逆风时往往会用披水板配合帆和舵作调戗航行，逆风调戗时的披水板操作方法就是轮流放下下风侧的披水板。

Leeboard

A leeboard was a stabilizing attachment on the sand junk, used to prevent leeway. It was also known as quarter board and commonly called "Tou Qiao" in the Ming and Qing Dynasties. A leeboard was usually a rectangular piece of hardwood, usually made of lithocarpus, chestnut and beech, slightly narrower in the upper and wider in the lower part, its length equal to the width of junk, and its thickness varying depending on its length. In general, leeboards are installed on both sides in front of the mainmast on a double-masted Sha Chuan, and at 2/5 of the whole length from the stern. They functioned as follows: when the junk had the wind coming from one side, the leeboards set on the downwind side were lowered in turn to reduce or prevent leeway and help keep the course over the ground close to the course steered. Generally, large and medium-sized junks would employ a pulley system to hoist and lower the leeboards, which could be extremely heavy.

披水板 | Leeboard

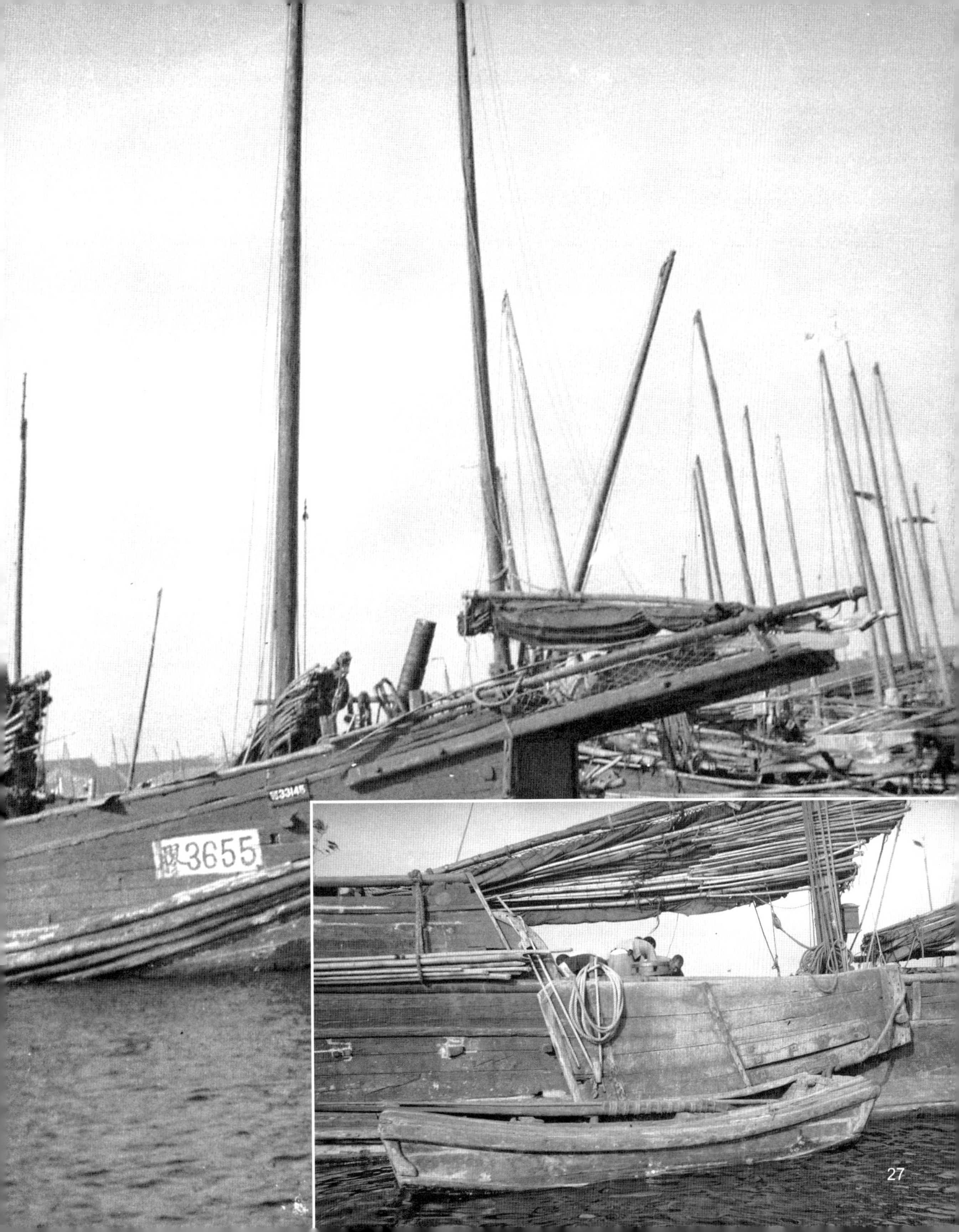
3655

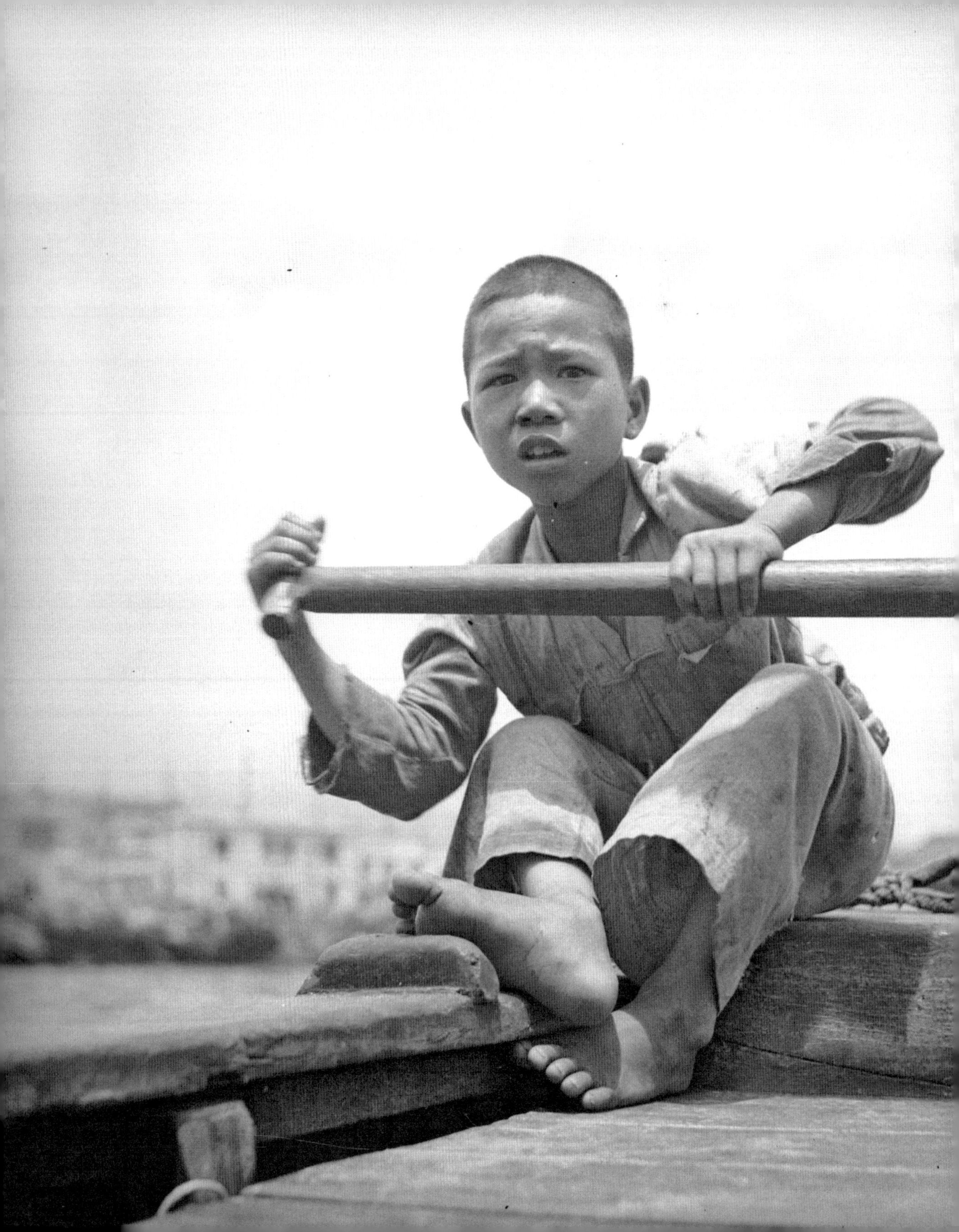

上　海
Shanghai

上海港 | Shanghai Port

"我爹爹一直在船上工作，他告诉我在船上吃鱼的时候不能把鱼翻过来，而且还要从上吃到下，要不然船会翻掉，不吉利。还有'篙子'（筷子），爸爸说了不能放在碗上，说是船会搁浅的。"

——上海舢板男孩

"My Dad has been working on board, he told me that fish cannot be turned over while eating, otherwise the ship will reverse, and that is unlucky. And chopsticks cannot be put on the bowl, that means that the boat will be stranded."

— Boy on sampan from Shanghai

上海港

上海港位于长江三角洲前缘,地处中国大陆海岸线的中部,扼居长江入海口,是我国沿海的主枢纽港和长江航运的重要港口。上海港依江临海,以上海为依托、长江流域为后盾,有着广阔而富庶的经济腹地,航线贯通南北、遍布世界。1843年11月,上海港被迫对外开放。19世纪70年代,发展成为全国的航运中心。20世纪30年代,成为远东航运中心,年货物吞吐量一度高达1400万吨。沙船是上海港近海及内水航运的主要船型。

上海港 | Shanghai Port

Shanghai Port

Shanghai Port is on the east side of the Yangtze River Delta. It occupies the central part of China's mainland coastal line and the estuary where the Yangtze River debouches into the sea, and become the heart of the country's coastal and Yangtze River shipping. With this great geographic advantage, Shanghai has a vast and fertile hinterland and its shipping route extends not only into inland China but also around the whole world. In November of 1843, Shanghai was forced to open up a treaty port. However, in only 30 years it had rapidly developed into the centre of China's shipping system. Later Shanghai became the shipping centre of the Far East in the 1930s, with a maximum annual cargo handling capacity of 14 million tons. The typical type of junk in Shanghai Port was the sand junk, which was widely used in coastal and inland waters.

舢舨

舢舨，又称舢板或三板，是一种广为使用的木板船，通常用于捕鱼或接驳。各地舢板的构造略有差别。上海地区的舢板，通常又称为"划子"，船体最初由底板和两侧舷板组成，而后又吸收了海船形制，船尾向上弯曲，艉板上增加横梁，船上架橹，摇橹时能产生较大的推力，还能用来操控航向，可以适应狭窄航道的航行。船上可携带简单的炊具，一家人就在船上狭小的空间内起居生活。

舢舨-1 | Sampan-1

舢舨-2 | Sampan-2

Sampan

Sampan, also known as "Shan Ban"（舢板）or "San Ban"（三板）, was a small wooden watercraft widely used for fishing or as a tender. Sampans from different regions vary considerably in form and construction. The Shanghai sampan was also commonly known as "Hua Zi" [literally "little row (boat)"]. The hull originally consisted of a flat bottom and side boards, later adapted to a more typical boat hull form. It featured an overhanging stern that curves upward, a transom across the stern, propelled by powerful yulohs (sculling oars), which also did the steering. This type of craft was well adapted to the narrow waterways of inland and coastal navigation. Using simple cooking equipment, families lived in the small spaces of some examples.

櫓 | Yuloh (Sculling Oar)

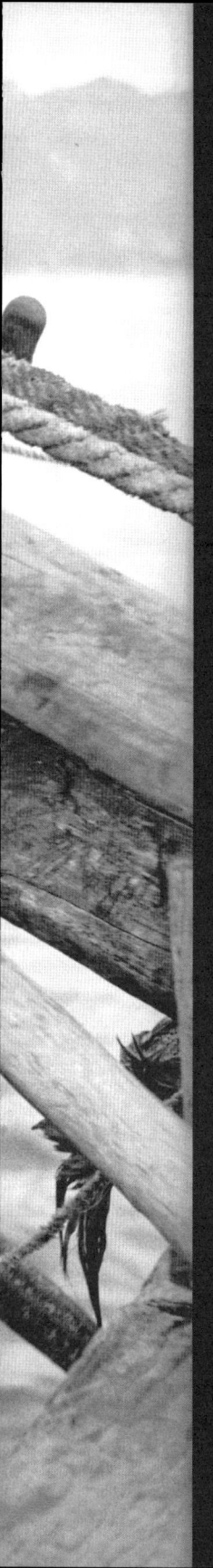

橹

橹是中国古船中普遍使用的一类集推进和操纵功能于一身的船舶属具,汉代时就已出现,在内河和沿海都得到广泛应用。橹由橹板、橹柄以及将二者连接起来的"二壮"构成,一般用杉木、松木、稠木制成,橹板横剖面通常呈圆背形,入水部分渐宽而薄,橹柄横剖面一般为圆形。在船侧设置搁橹的支点,称为橹支纽或橹人头,又以一根粗绳(又称橹索)将橹柄顶端与甲板上的铁环相连,形成一个摇橹系统。橹是纵向布置,左右摇动橹柄,橹以橹支纽为支点充分转动,摇橹者既可以调整橹板划水时的攻角,用力小效率高,又可以调节橹与船舶中线面的角度,操纵和控制船舶的航向。又由于摇橹时橹板不出水面而能连续工作,使得橹的推进效率很高,在一些大船上有使用 20 支橹的,元、明时期最大的海船上有时约有 30 支橹同时操作,小型海船常用 2 支橹。

Yuloh (Sculling Oar)

Yulohs were commonly used both for propulsion and steering in Chinese junks. The first yulohs were thought to have appeared in the Han Dynasty and widely used inland as well as in coastal waters. A yuloh was made up of blade, shaft, the handle section and the "Er Zhuang". The "Er Zhuang" was the critical part connecting the blade and handle so that the resultant loom of the oar was kinked. A yuloh was generally made of fir, pine or other wood. The cross section of the yuloh board usually had a circular back while that of the yuloh shaft was round. The immersion part of the yuloh board became wider and thinner. The yuloh operated by being balanced on a pivot or "Ren Tou". A strong rope (also known as the yuloh rope) connected the head of the handle to an iron hoop on the deck, forming a complete system. The yuloh worked by being pushed and pulled horizontally so that the whole mechanism rotated a quarter to a half a turn at the end of each stroke, the system being semi-automatic as a result of the yuloh rope and the pivot. With the angle of attack of the blade adjusted by the rower, the vessel's speed and heading could be efficiently controlled. The efficiency of yulohs meant that large junks could be propelled by just twenty to thirty pairs. In the Yuan and Ming Dynasties, the biggest junk sometimes employed about 30 yulohs, but after the Ming Dynasty, small-sized marine junks had only two.

崇明运棉船-1、2
Chongming Cotton Junk-1、2

崇明运棉船

崇明运棉船往返于黄浦江,航行路线从长江口的崇明岛至上海,主要运载棉花和旅客。运棉船一般用质地松软的松木建造,外观上崇明运棉船与北直隶商船相似,船长约 12~18 米,宽不超过 2.1~2.4 米,甲板为平铺式,船上一般立两桅或三桅,主桅高立于船舯,悬挂普通直纵帆,大风袭来时只需把主升降绳一松就能迅速落帆,既保证了船只在微风中有足够的动力,又能快速有效地应对大风突袭。

Chongming Cotton Junk

The Chongming cotton junk was employed on round trips via the Huangpu River, sailing from Chongming Island at the mouth of the Yangtze River to Shanghai, mainly carrying cotton and passengers. It was usually built with pinewood, with an appearance that resembled a small Beizhili trading junk. The junk's length was about 12~18 metres and its beam no more than 2.1~2.4 metres. It had a flat planked deck and two or three masts. The mainmast stood amidships with a normal fore-and-aft sails. If the wind got up the crew only needed to loose the halyard to drop the sail. This arrangement guaranteed enough power to sail as well as an ability to douse sail quickly when needed.

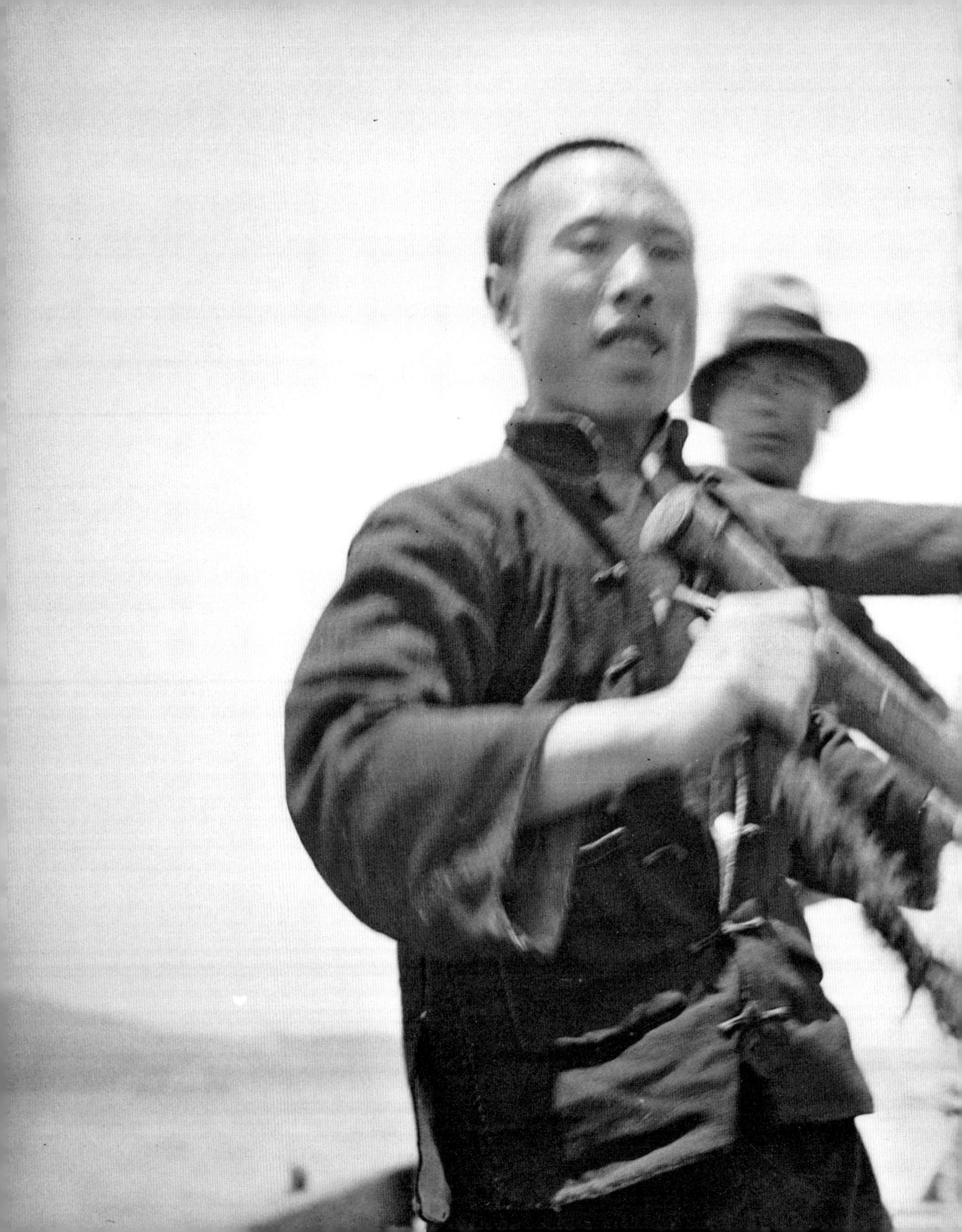

浙 江
Zhejiang

宁波港 | Ningbo Port

"我们家的新船是在舟山打的,下水第一件事就是开着新船到普陀山进香拜佛,回来时带了点山花、山柴、桃枝,这些叫'顺风柴',插在船头、船后轿以避邪讨吉利。"

——宁波船主

"Our new junk was competed in Zhoushan Islands. After the launching ceremony, I set my first sail to Mount Putuo to burn incense and pray, and returned with flowers, firewood and peach branches—these are called 'Wind Firewood', I insert these in the bow and stern, to avoid evil and pray for the good luck."

—Ship owner from Ningbo

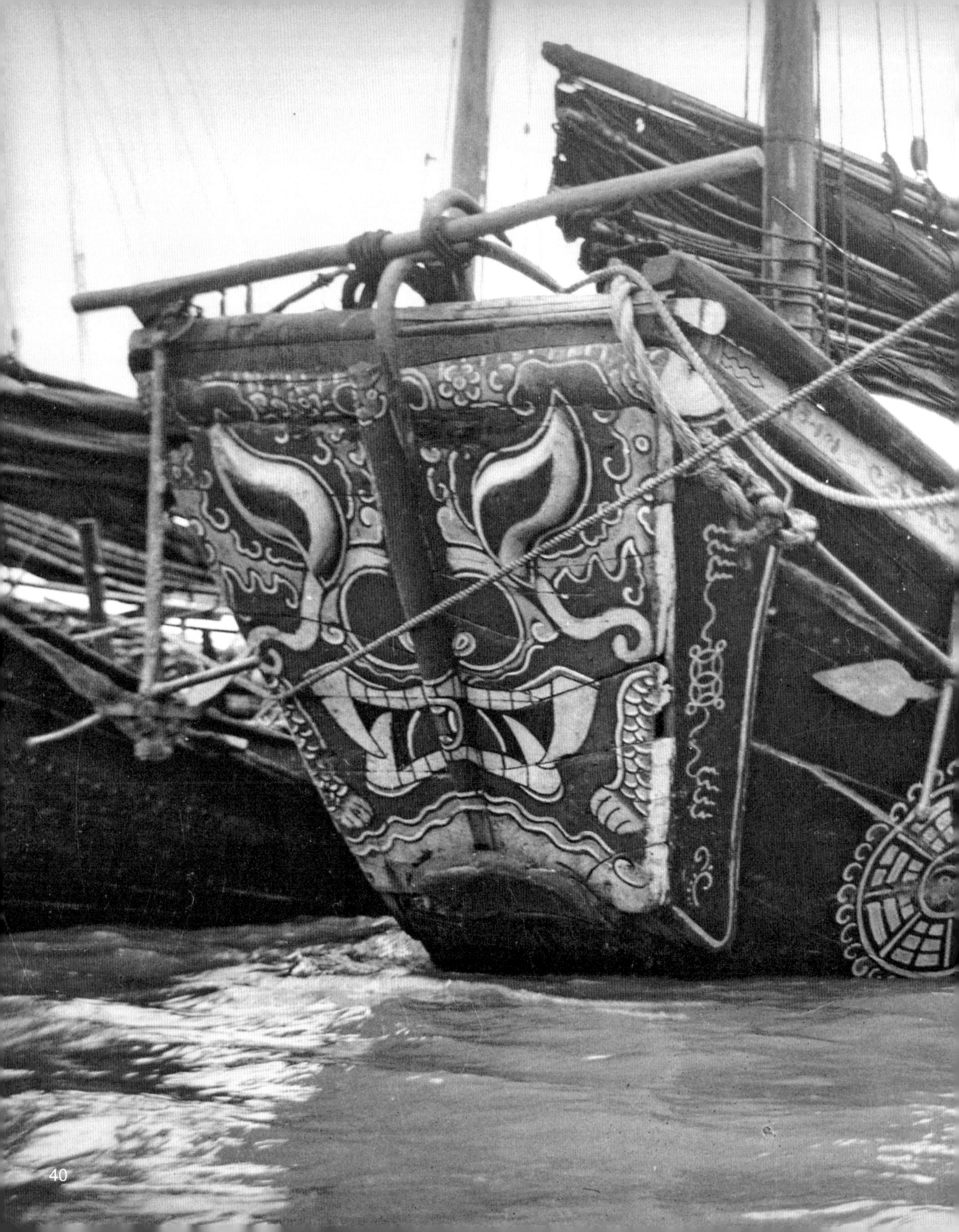

杭州湾商船

杭州湾商船行驶于杭州湾南岸各港，亦称绍兴船，主要从浙江各港运送柴火、木炭和棉花到上海。商船的装饰十分华丽，船身涂满了鲜艳的色块和图案，主色调以红、蓝为主。船艏绘有五官夸张的龙头、虎头或脸谱图案，后跟着两个八卦；船艉以同样鲜明的色彩描绘一对凤凰，船艉侧板还会根据船主喜好绘有观音、八仙等人物。商船的主要结构特点是：采用箱形结构，船头较平且向前倾，船艉板呈四方形，甲板平铺；船体为平底，被分隔成若干隔舱；长度可达300米，有3根桅杆，可载重百吨以上。

Hangzhou Bay Trading Junk

Hangzhou Bay trading junks travelled along the ports on the south shore of Hangzhou Bay. They were also known as Shaoxing junks and mainly transported firewood, charcoal and cotton from Zhejiang ports to Shanghai. They were gaily decorated with bright colours and patterns, primarily in red and blue. The bow was painted with exaggerated features like a dragon's head, tiger head or mask. On each bow at the side were two "Ba Gua" (the auspicious octagon with the eight Taoist symbols or trigrams representing the fundamental principles of reality). Also, the quarters displayed two vividly coloured phoenixes, one on each side. Other patterns could be commonly found depending on the owner's preferences, like *Guanyin* or the Eight Immortals from the Chinese mythology. The junk's main features included the use of a box-shaped structure, a flat bow inclined forward, a square transom, planked deck, a flat bottomed hull, and the usual internal division into several compartments. It could measure up to 30 metres in length, with 3 masts, capable of hauling above one hundred tons.

杭州湾商船-1
Hangzhou Bay Trading Junk-

杭州湾商船-2 | Hangzhou Bay Trading Junk-2

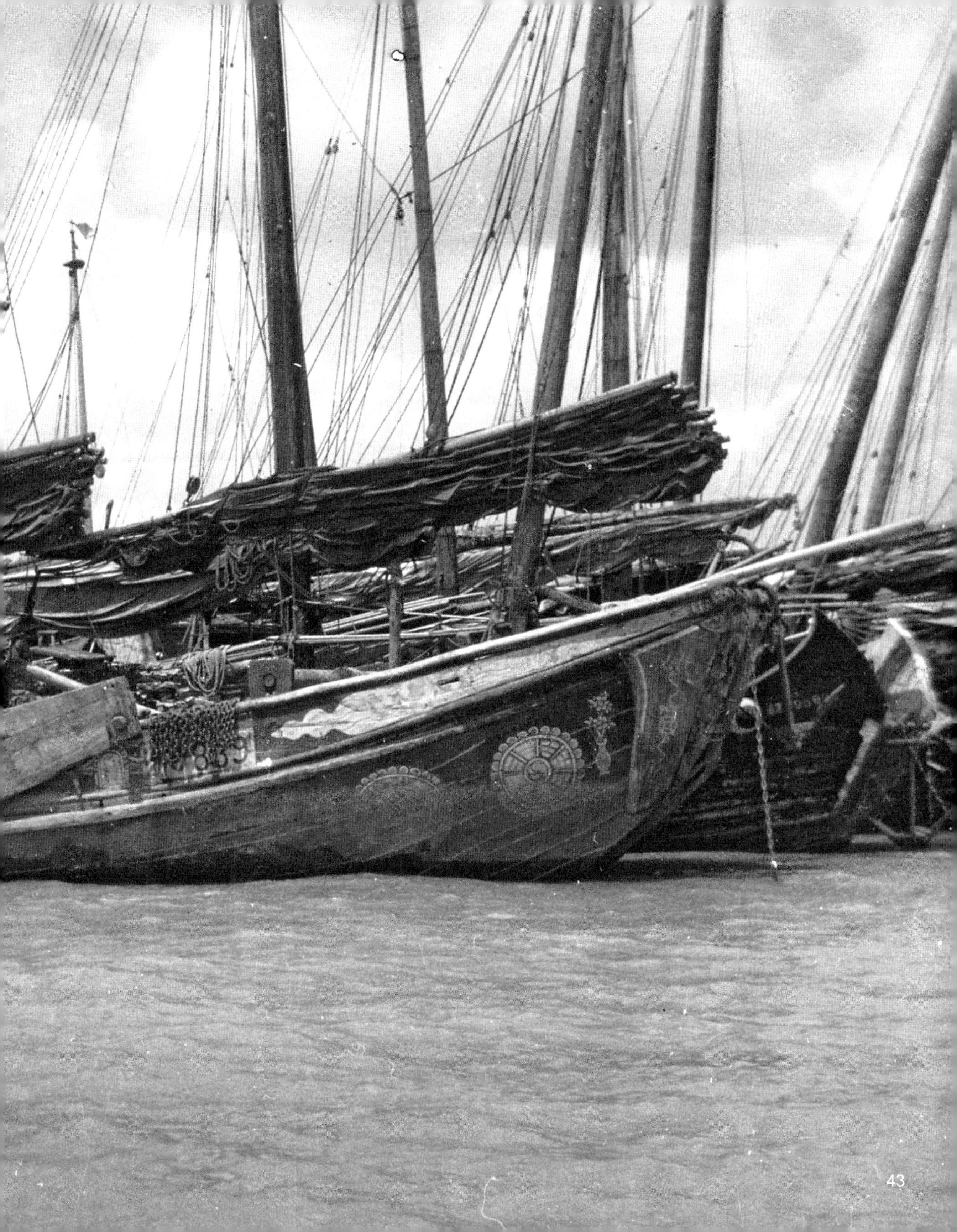

44

船艏/船舻图案

中国部分古船的外表经过刷漆处理后,还会用漆画进行装饰。日本长崎平户市松浦史料馆收藏的《唐船图》中所描绘的商船船图,记录了明清时期商船用漆装饰的历史面貌。因为中国北方木帆船都是方头且向前倾的缘故,首封板设计成了中国古船的特点之一,上面常绘有鹢鸟、虎等动物形象,称为"船头像",有的还绘有阴阳图、脸谱等。清代雍正年间为了对各省商船进行区别,规定各省商船自船头至大桅处的横梁及大桅的一半涂以特定色彩,"广船粉红,福船涂绿,浙船油白,江船漆蓝",于是便有了红头船、绿头船、白头船和蓝头船的说法。

Patterns on Bow and Stern

Some Chinese ancient junks had wood treatment and were painted decoratively. The decorations on trading junks in the Ming and Qing Dynasties were vividly recorded in the *Tangchuan Tu* Paintings, collected in the Matsuura Historical Museum in Hirado, Nagasaki, Japan. Because the wooden ships in north China normally had forward inclined square bows, bow plate designs became one of their main characteristics. Bows were often painted with animal features like birds and tigers, called "bow decorations", some with the Yin-Yang Pattern, with masks and so on. During the reign of Emperor Yongzheng of the Qing Dynasty, in order to distinguish provincial trading junks, they were painted specific colours on the beam from bow to mainmast, and over half of the mainmast: Canton junks in pink, Fuzhou pole junks in green, Zhejiang junks in white, river junks in blue. The result were so-called red-head junks, green-head junks, white-head junks and blue-head junks.

船艏/舻图案船-1、2
Patterns on Bow and Stern-1、2

宁波港

宁波港是我国古代"海上丝绸之路"始发港之一，位于浙江东北部，地处中国海岸线中段、长江三角洲南翼，扼居南北水路之要冲，东有舟山群岛作为天然屏障。宁波港水域广深，不冻不淤，终年通航，是我国历史上对外贸易的重要港口和海运中转枢纽。春秋时期称句章港，唐代称明州港，元代称庆元港，明代始称宁波港。疍船（通称宁船）是宁波港的特定船型，港内也有浙江本省及周边各地开来的各式海船，还有数量众多的内河船。

宁波港 | Ningbo Port

Ningbo Port

Ningbo Port was one of the departure ports of the Chinese Ancient "Maritime Silk Road". It is located in the northeast of Zhejiang Province, sheltered by the Zhoushan Islands in the east and occupies the middle of China's coastal line and the south wing of Yangtze Delta. Thus the port plays an important role in inland north-south waterways. Ningbo Port is famous for its wide harbour and deep waters with no siltation or ice, which makes it navigable all year around. It was a key port of foreign trade and a transit station of maritime transportation in China's history. It was firstly named Gouzhang Port in the Spring and Autumn Period, then in the Tang Dynasty it changed its name to Mingzhou Port, and Qingyuan Port in the Yuan Dynasty. The name Ningbo was finally determined in the Ming Dynasty. The specific ship type of Ningbo Port was the Dan Chuan, more widely known as Ning Chuan (Ningbo junk). In addition, the port harboured sea-going junks from nearby and different regions in Zhejiang as well as a large number of river-borne vessels.

绿眉毛船（舟山船）-1 | Green Eyebrow (Zhoushan) Junk-1

绿眉毛船（舟山船）

绿眉毛船因船眼上方会漆一条绿漆，形状类似眉毛而得名，属于舟山船型。舟山船来自上海、浙江各港及舟山群岛，可分为渔船和商船两类。从外观看，商船和渔船并无太大差异，但大小差异悬殊，最大的可载运百吨，最小只能载运 10 吨。这类船的典型特征是船舯为开放式，且船舯位置的舷墙呈弧形向外翻；船艉呈马蹄形，

Green Eyebrow (Zhoushan) Junk

The green eyebrow junk gained its names from the shape of the green painted bow above its oculus, which looks like an eyebrow. It was one of the junks that came from Shanghai, other Zhejiang ports and from the Zhoushan Islands. These could be divided into fishing junks and trading junks. However, in terms of their appearance they did not differ that much although they did differ greatly in size. The largest junks carried hundreds of tons whilst the smallest could carry only about 10 tons. The design was typically characterized by an open bow, outwardly curved bulwarks on each bow, and a horseshoe-shaped stern, with high bulwarks along both sides to ensure dry decks at sea. The type had three masts with the standard junk's fully battened, balanced lug sails.

绿眉毛船(舟山船)-2 | Green Eyebrow (Zhoushan) Junk-2

绿眉毛船（舟山船）-3 | Green Eyebrow (Zhoushan) Junk-3

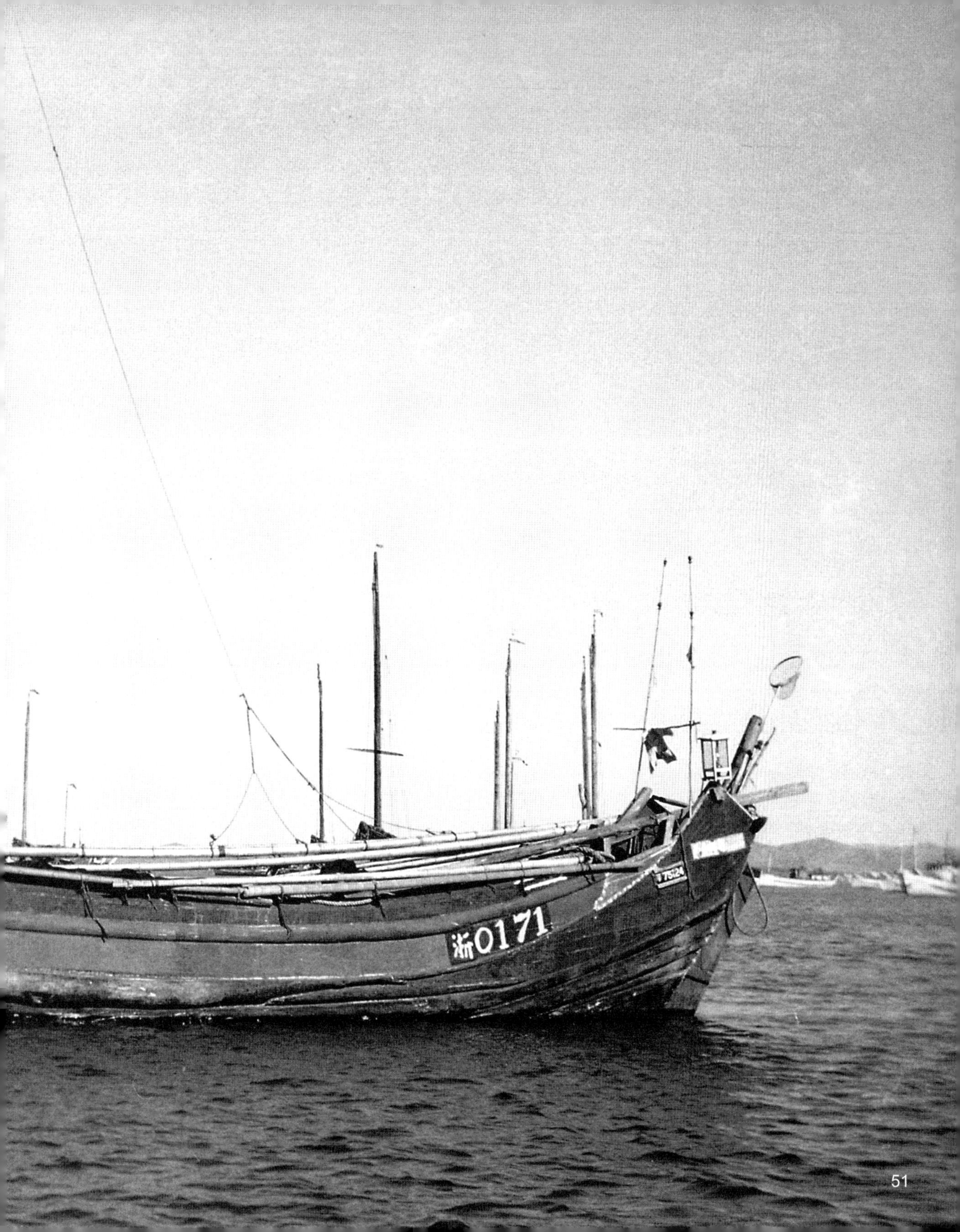
浙0171

船帆

船帆为推进工具，中国式船帆战国时就已出现，在汉代得到广泛应用，宋代时得以进一步改进。中国式船帆基本可分为梯形帆、斜桁帆和扇形帆。早期船帆用植物叶或竹篾编织而成，称为硬帆，当船帆由竹篾过渡到布帆时，则在纵帆上设置很多横向的帆竹（横桁）。当船帆受到不同方向的风吹袭时，横桁的作用是使得帆的形状不会发生太大变化，也相当于硬帆。中国式船帆最大的特点不仅是硬帆，而且帆面可作大角度的转动，因此它可以利用八面来风，即使遇到斜逆风或顶头风，也可以调戗使船走"之"字形航行。其另一个特点是帆面可以升降，扬帆时需要多人合力且经常要使用扬帆绞车，但遇到狂风时则可以迅速落帆保证安全。为了调控船帆，中国人还发明出了一系列索具，如吊帆索、拉帆索、抱桅索、控帆索、提头索、脚索等。

Sail

The sail is thought to have appeared as a propulsion method during the Warring States Period, to have become widely used later in the Han Dynasty, and further improved in the Song Dynasty. China's junk sails could be divided into three types: the lugsail, the spritsail and the fan-shaped sail. In early times, sail fabric was a sandwich of woven leaves between open woven rattan panels, to create a series of solid panels one above the other. Later, when canvas appeared, bamboo battens replaced the earlier panel junctions stretching across the sail's full width. Whatever the prevailing winds were in a voyaging area, the battens kept the shape of the multiple panels under control, working in theory as a solid panel. Like all sails, the junk sail had a wide range of rotation so as to take advantage of the direction of the wind. In principle because it was an unstayed, fore-and-aft rig, the junk sail could be trimmed to tack upwind or headwind. Another unique feature was that the sail could also be raised or lowered. These fairly crudely built battened sails were heavy. On larger junks it took several people to hoist the sail, even using the simple horizontal barrel winches. However, the heavy sail had the advantage that it could be dropped quickly in strong winds: a major safety feature. There was a full range of running rigging such as sail hoist rope, sail pull rope, mast hold rope, sail control rope, lifting head rope and footrope to control the sails.

船帆 | Sail

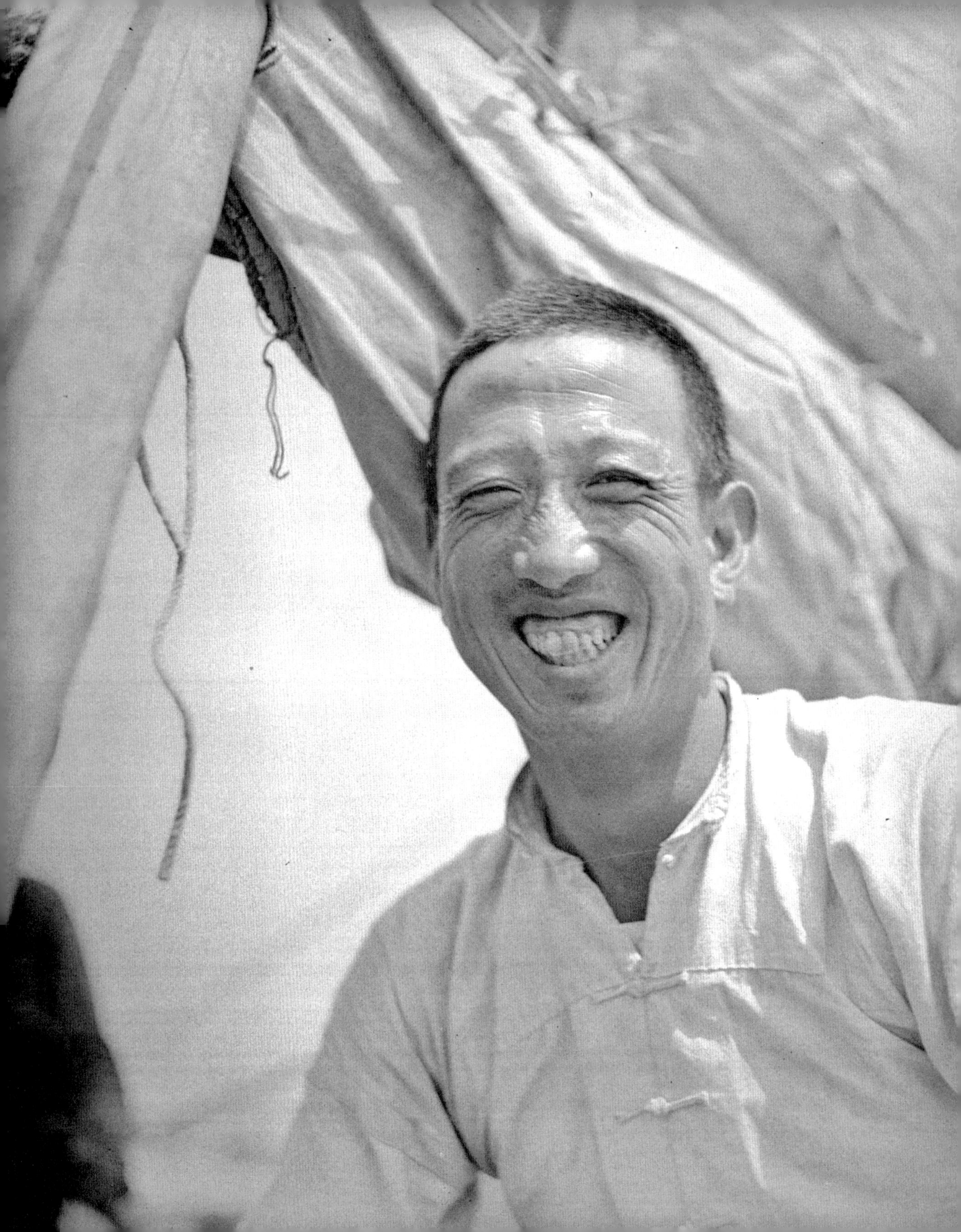

福建
Fujian

泉州港 | Quanzhou Port
厦门港 | Xiamen (Amoy) Port

"天黑黑要落雨,海王船要出岛。阿爸出海去讨鱼,阿母烧船送王船。一送金银和财宝,二送粮草摆酒席,三送神明去护保。"

——福建渔民

"It's getting dark, rain comes. Abba (Dad) is about to set sail for fishing, Ammu (Mum) is burning a ship model to pray, sending gold and treasures, sending food and feast, and sending gods to protect."

—Fisherman from Fujian

泉州港-1、2 | Quanzhou Port-1、2

泉州港

泉州港，古称"刺桐港"，是我国古代"海上丝绸之路"始发港之一，位于福建东南海滨，地处晋江入海口。泉州港，兴于唐代；宋元时期，得以迅速发展，被誉为"东方第一大港"；元末，由于社会动乱不安，泉州港渐衰；明清时期，急剧走向衰落。泉州港位居东海航线与南海航线的交汇点，往南可前往菲律宾、印度尼西亚等地；往东可至日本；往北可到朝鲜；在沿海一带又可以南通广州，北到宁波。

Quanzhou Port

Quanzhou Port was known in ancient times as Citong Port and was one of the departure ports in the Chinese Ancient "Maritime Silk Road". It was located on the southeast coast of Fujian Province, on the estuary of the Jin River. Quanzhou originated in the Tang Dynasty, and experienced a rapid development in the Song and Yuan Dynasties. During this period the port was praised as the biggest port in the east. However, due to social unrest, Quanzhou Port gradually fell into decay in the late Yuan Dynasty and finally dramatically declined in the Ming and Qing Dynasties. Quanzhou was at the junction of the east route and the south route for traditional Chinese trading voyages. The south route led across the South China Sea to the Philippines, Indonesia and other places. The east route reached Japan and the north to Korea. Guangzhou and Ningbo were on the coastal routes to either side.

泉州商船

泉州商船往返于泉州等福建港口以及上海等北方港口之间，被当地人称为"白底船"。这种船操纵灵活，长约22.5米，宽约4.5米，船艏型线瘦长，入水处尖削，船艉型线平缓，但船舯下凹的弧度较大。船艉呈椭圆形，有船艉板，艉翼板稍稍伸出船艉。出海时，靠着装置在船艉的绞辘，舵可以放入水中，低于船底，大大提升了舵效。

Quanzhou Trading Junk

The Quanzhou trading junk worked between Fujian ports and as far north as Shanghai. It was also known locally as "the white-bottom junk". It was an adaptable design, about 22.5 metres long and 4.5 metres in beam, with a bow that narrowed towards a sharp cutwater at the waterline. The stern was flat and the hull had a pronounced sheer. The stern was oval with rear wing panels stretching slightly beyond the transom. The rudder was raised and lowered by a windlass at the stern and could be lowered below the line of the keel to markedly reduce leeway.

泉州商船 | Quanzhou Trading Junk

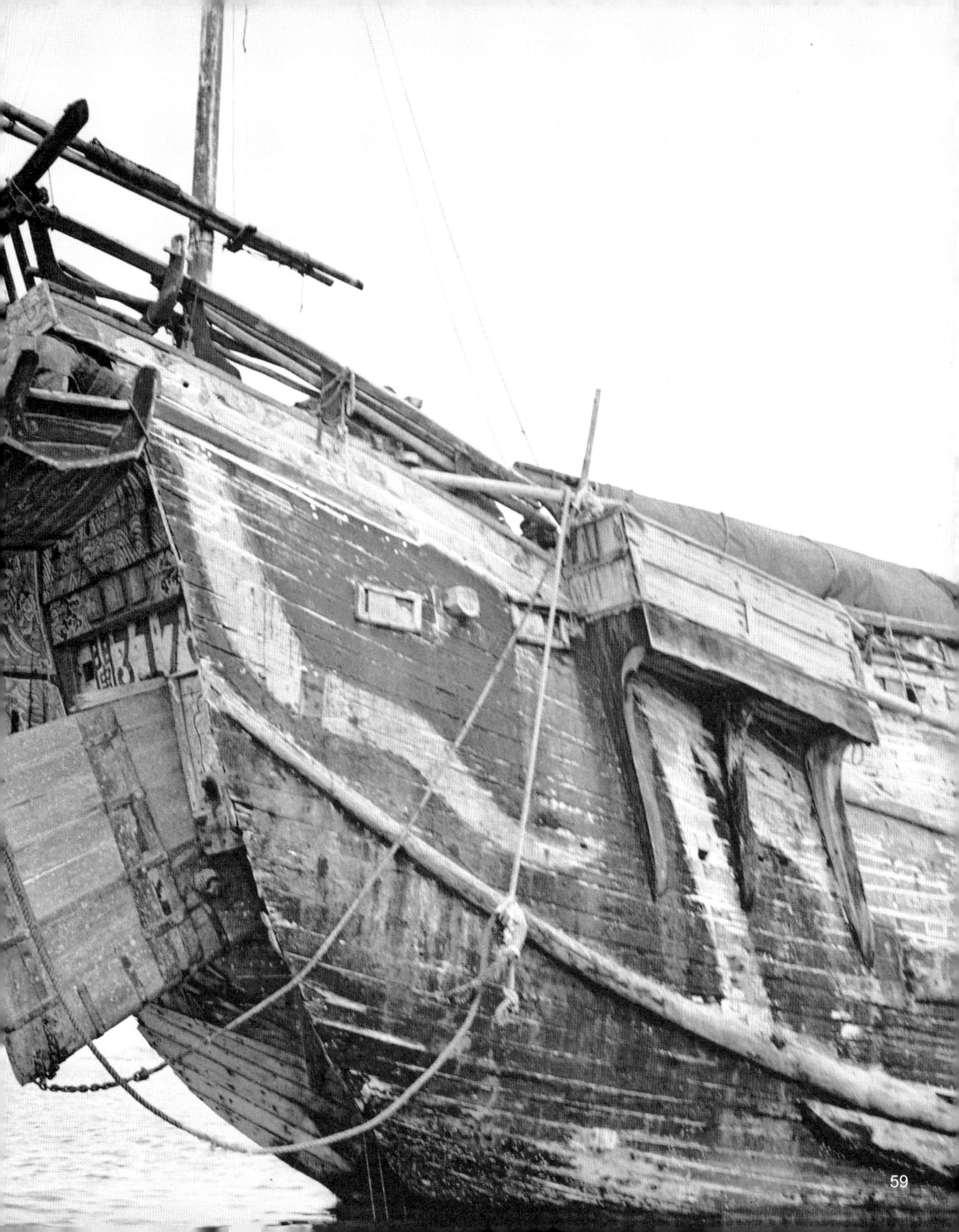

厦门港

厦门港位于福建东南的金门湾内、九龙江入海口，地处漳州、泉州之间，濒临台湾海峡，为我国东南海疆之要津，入闽之门户，也是闽南金三角的中心。1842年，《南京条约》签订后，被辟为五个通商口岸之一。20世纪30年代前后，新建大小码头28座，港口繁荣兴盛。从厦门北航的船舶主要是"贩艚船"，又称作"北艚船"；南航的主要为"南艚船"；对渡台湾航线上的海船被通称为"横洋船"。

Xiamen(Amoy) Port

Xiamen Port is located inside the Golden Gate Bay in the southeast of Fujian Province and is in the estuary of Jiujiang River. With its location between Zhangzhou and Quanzhou, neighbouring the Taiwan Strait, Xiamen Port becomes the key port of China's southeast sea, the entrance into the Fujian Province and the economic centre of the Golden Delta in southern Fujian Province. After the signing of the Treaty of Nanjing in 1842, Xiamen was opened up as one of the five treaty ports. It soon developed and later the port flourished in the 1930s with 28 wharfs in different scales. The main junks sailing to the north in Xiamen Port was the Fancao Chuan, also known as Beicao Chuan; the ones sailing to the south called Nancao Chuan; those sailing to Taiwan were named Hengyang Chuan.

厦门港 | Xiamen (Amoy) Port

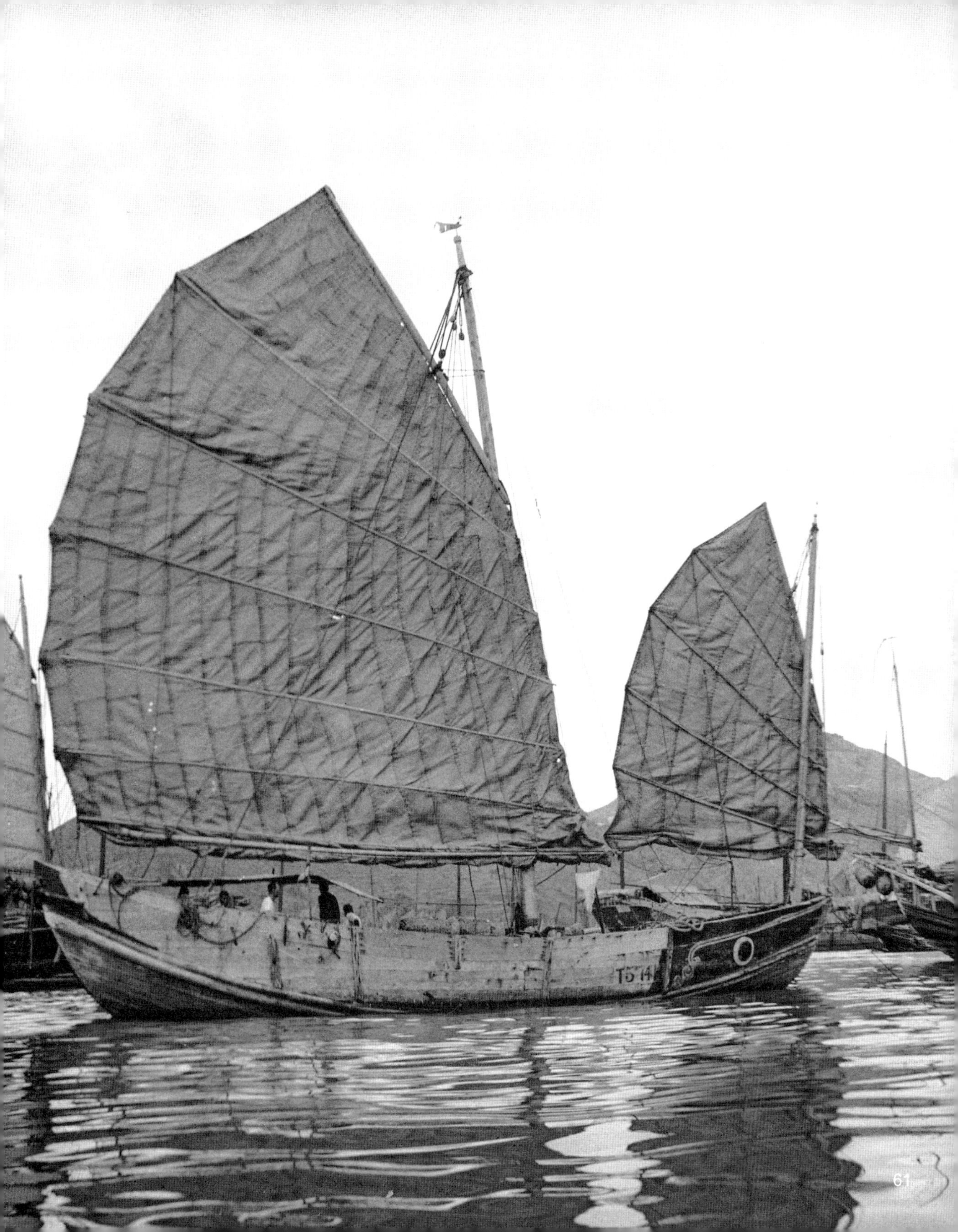

厦门商船

厦门商船出自漳州，但主港在厦门，航行于厦门、台湾、上海和华南各港，也常见于海南和中南半岛各港，载重量可达 150 吨。外观上与其他福建商船无太大区别。船舯为开口式，型线和缓，较为瘦窄，船艉呈椭圆形，船艉板至水线之间横架一块厚木，设有舵杆孔悬着舵，在海上航行时舵从舵杆孔沉入水底。厦门商船的装饰与渔船一样，船头板上部漆黑色并绘阴阳图，下部漆红色，中央黑红相接处以新月形图案分开。

Xiamen (Amoy) Trading Junk

This type of junk loaded up to 150 tons, and came from Zhangzhou, but their main port could have been Xiamen. They were generally seen in Xiamen, Taiwan, Shanghai and south China, as well as other ports in Hainan and Indo-china. Their appearance shared very similar characteristics with Fujian trading junks. The bow was open, the sheer was gentle and the hull was narrow beamed. The oval-shaped stern had a heavy wooden bar set horizontally between the transom and waterline on which the rudder was mounted. The rudder was lowered below the waterline when sailing. The decoration of these Xiamen trading junks was the same as the fishing ones. The upper bow plate was painted black with a Yin-Yang Pattern. The bottom of the bow was painted red and the two parts were separated by a crescent pattern in the middle.

厦门商船 | Xiamen (Amoy) Trading Junk

厦门渔船

厦门渔船作业于天气恶劣、风暴较多的台湾海峡。该渔船结构牢固且速度较快,没有舷墙,船舷至船艉的弧度较大。船艏尖削,船艉与泉州商船类似,有升降舵。厦门渔船通常是两桅。它的船帆很有特色,帆身较高,前缘和下风缘笔直,一般用15~20根竹撑条支撑,是长江口以南唯一采用这种帆的船型。其装饰亦引人注目,船头板上部漆黑色并绘阴阳图,下部漆红色,中央黑红相接处以新月型图案分开。船侧厚板以下漆白漆、以上漆红漆起保护作用。

Xiamen (Amoy) Fishing Junk

Xiamen fishing junks operated in the Taiwan Strait, where there was strong winds and frequent storms. There were strongly built without any bulwarks with a marked sheer. They were reputed to sail fast. They had a more pointed bow and a stern similar to the Quanzhou trading junk, mounted with a hoistable rudder. It usually had two masts, and a very characteristic sail with a high peak and a straight luff and leech, with 15~20 bamboo battens. There were the only junk that employed this type of sail in the south of the Yangtze River estuary. There were also appealingly decorated like the trading junks, with the upper bow transom painted black with the Yin-Yang Pattern, the bottom painted red, and the two parts were separated by a pattern of the crescent in the middle. Below the side plate the junk was white, and above this was red for protection.

厦门渔船 | Xiamen (Amoy) Fishing Junk

厦门盐船

厦门盐船应属于福船中主要用于运输货物的贩艚船,一般需要按照政府规定的船型制造,具备福船的基本特征。一般船体较大,有相当的载重量,可载盐100吨。根据船体各部件的不同要求,选择木质轻重不同的木材。船为尖底,采用纵向的龙骨,船艏较尖,尾部较宽,艏艉呈较大的弧形。

Xiamen (Amoy) Salt Junk

The Xiamen salt junk belonged to the Fancao Chuan type, which was categorized as a pole junk and mainly used for the transport of goods. Its structure was manufactured in accordance with the government's requirement, and it showed basic features of pole junks. Thus it had a large hull with the considerable load capacity to carry 100 tons of salt. Various timber types were used for different parts of the hull. The junk had sharp deadrise, a Fujian-type keel, was narrower forward than aft, and had a marked sheer.

厦门盐船-1、2 | Xiamen (Amoy) Salt Junk-1、2

68

船眼

明清时期，中国古船装饰中出现了一种独特的"船眼"装饰，即在船头描绘一对大大的眼睛，由福建沿海传播到台湾雅美族的拼板木船至今仍保留在船的首尾雕刻齿轮状圆圈的习俗，雅美人亦称之为船眼。船眼一般出现在福船、广船、浙船的装饰中，福船在造船开眼时还会有一套祭奠仪式，在眼中钉三块红布。不同古船的"船眼"方向会有不同，一种解释认为与船的功能有关，眼睛向下看海的是渔船，这样能够观察到鱼虾，寓意获得丰收；眼睛平视远方的是商船，寓意可以顺利抵达港口；眼睛向上的则是官船，寓意官员高升。

Ship's Eye (Oculus)

In the Ming and Qing Dynasties, a unique decoration emerged called the "ship's eye" (oculus), which depicted a pair of large eyes on the stern. The wooden jointed-board boats built by the Yami ethnic group had preserved the custom of carving a gear-shaped circle on either side of the bow and the Yami called this the ship's eye. The oculus was generally seen in the decorations of the pole junk, Guangdong junk and junks from Zhejiang Province. There was even a memorial ceremony of nailing up three red cloths during the opening of the oculus when building pole junk. The directions of different junks also differ depending on their functions. It was said that junks with oculus looking down were fishing junks hoping for a good harvest, junks with the oculus looking at the distance were trading junks hoping for smooth arrival and junks with oculus looking upward were official junks hoping for a rise in position.

花屁股船

花屁股船即福州杉船,被称为杉船是因为其专门运送杉木,被称为花屁股船可能是因船艉会装饰颜色鲜艳的图案,不同的村、港口可能有不同的装饰图案。福州杉船从福州出发,沿着海岸南北向航行。这种船一般长 36~54 米,宽 6.6~8.4 米,载重量约 180~400 吨,可容纳 25~35 名船员。船上有 3 根桅杆,前桅前倾,立于船眼,主桅竖立在船舯,艉桅稍偏离中线,立于艉楼后侧,桅上悬挂用撑条支撑加固的斜桁帆。该船有水密隔舱系统,两道横向和纵向的隔墙又将隔舱分成若干小舱。从福州到上海沿途浅滩较多,因此船底平面较大。杉船船艏十分独特,为开放性船艏,两侧的翼板弯曲成尖角,像鸟嘴。这样的船艏与装置升降舵的船艉相配合,使船在航行时能保持较好的稳定性。因为杉船专为运载杉木而建造,所以船舯和船艉向内倾斜较大,杉木架于两侧,即方便装卸,又能防风浪。

Flowery Stern (Hua Pi Gu) Junk

A flowery stern junk was a actually Fuzhou fir-carrying junk. The fir, or pole junk name came from its function of transporting fir poles in great bundles outboard on each side. It was called "Hua Pi Gu" because of the gaily decorated stern with colourful patterns that varied in different villages and ports. This type of junk started from Fuzhou, sailing along the coast either to the north or south. Typical examples had 25~35 crew, were 36~54 metres in length, 6.6~8.4 metres in beam and could carry approximately 180~400 tons. There were 3 masts: a forward canted foremast in the eyes of the ship, the mainmast amidships and the mizzenmast offset slightly from the centreline at the aft end of the poop. The hull had the usual bulkhead subdivision with the compartments further divided into several cabins by two longitudinal walls. There were many shoals along the route from Fuzhou to Shanghai, and therefore the hull bottom was large and flat. The junk had a unique open bow, with both sides curved to form a sharp angle, like bird's beak. Matched with the stern, which was equipped with hoistable rudder, bows like this could help maintain stability while sailing. Because fir junks were constructed for carrying fir poles in bundles outboard on either side, the hull had a marked tumblehome to protect from waves as well as to facilitate loading and unloading.

花屁股船 | Flowery Stern (Hua Pi Gu) Junk

福船舵 | Stern Rudder

福船舵

船舵是控制航向并保证船舶操作灵活性的重要属具。舵在汉代时就已出现,一般位于船尾部,也称为船艉舵,到了宋代,船舵技术已经成熟。船舵与风帆配合使用,使船舶的航线大为扩展。中国古代海船常沿海岸行驶,因此大多采用升降舵,可根据水深变化而升降,即进入深水区时,可以将舵放到船底之下;进入浅水区时,则可以把舵提升上来以免触及海底,在锚泊时,如风向、转向不顺时也可将舵提出水面避免走锚受损。

Stern Rudder

The rudder controls a ship's course. It had appeared by the Han Dynasty and at that time was normally mounted at the stern. By the Song Dynasty, this technology had matured. Due to the combination of rudder and sail, the routes had been greatly extended. Ancient Chinese junks travelled along the coast, so most of them employed hoistable rudders, which could change according to depth. When sailing in deep water the rudder was lowered to below the bottom of the junk, while in shallow water, it could be hoisted to avoid touching the seabed. When the junk was at anchor, the rudder would also be lifted out of the water to reduce the likelihood of damage.

福船

福船是福建、浙江沿海一带尖底海船的统称,可分为渔船、商船和盐船,该称谓最早见于明万历年间。福建造船业历史悠久,可上溯至春秋时期,在宋代福州、兴化、泉州、漳州等地已成为重要的造船中心。宋船"上平如衡,下侧如刃,贵其破浪而行也"的特点为后世的福船奠定了技术基础。福船船体结构的主要特点为:采用纵向的主龙骨,有的渔船在鱼舱部位没有若干横向或纵向的水密隔舱,分割成若干鱼舱,装置可升降转动的舵,通常为3桅帆,船帆可以升降转动,载重量大,可进行远洋航行。福船所包含的船型和用途相当广泛,包括福船一号、福船二号、哨船(草撇船)、冬船(海沧船)、鸟船和快船等。鸟船又可分为开浪船和苍山船,苍山船在福船体系中最小,在内海航行很有优势。

Pole Junk

The seagoing junks along the coasts of Fujian and Zhejiang had a sharper deadrise to the bottom and were collectively categorized as Fuzhou pole junks. The junks were divided into fishing junks, trading junks and salt junks. The term was first seen during the reign of Emperor Wanli of the Ming Dynasty. Fujian has a long shipbuilding history that can be traced back to the Spring and Autumn Period. In the Song Dynasty, Fuzhou, Xinghua, Quanzhou, Zhangzhou and other places became important centres for shipbuilding. The features of the junks in the Song Dynasty, including the flat top and the sharp deadrise, had also laid the foundations for the pole junks of later generations. Their distinctive difference was in the keel timber. Occasionally, the watertight bulkheads could be divided into several fish-storage rooms. Pole junks had three masts and its hoistable sail could also be trimmed for sailing offshore. Pole junks covered a wide range of types and uses, including pole junk I, pole junk II, Shao Chuan (Caopie Chuan), Dong Chuan (Haicang Chuan), Niao Chuan and Kuai Chuan. Niao Chuan could be further divided into Kailang Chuan and Cangshan Chuan. The Cangshan Chuan was the smallest in size among all the pole junks, but its basic design properties enabled it to sail well offshore despite its size.

福船-1 | Pole Junk-1

75

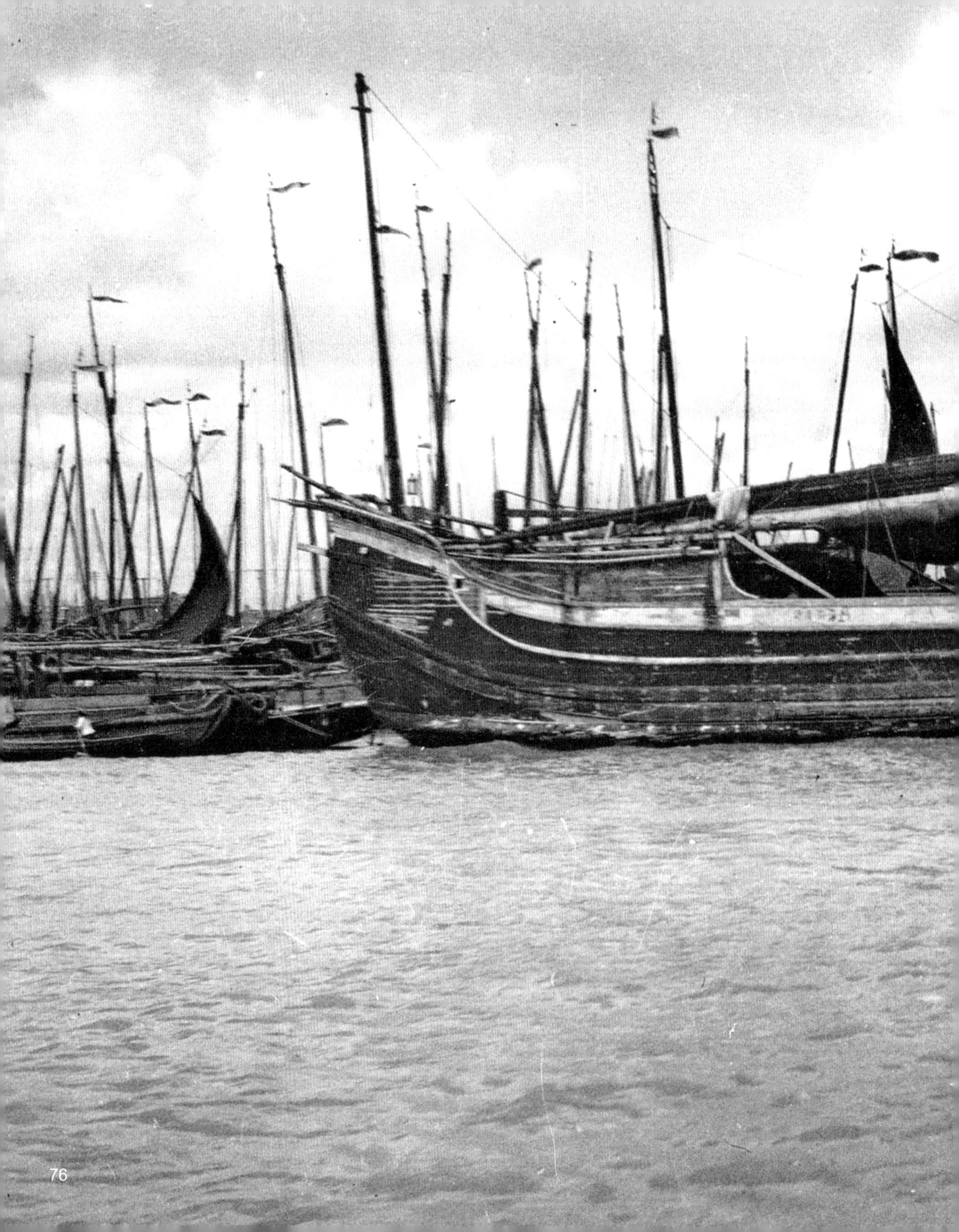

福船-2 | Pole Junk-2

福船-3 | Pole Junk-3

福船-4 | Pole Junk-4

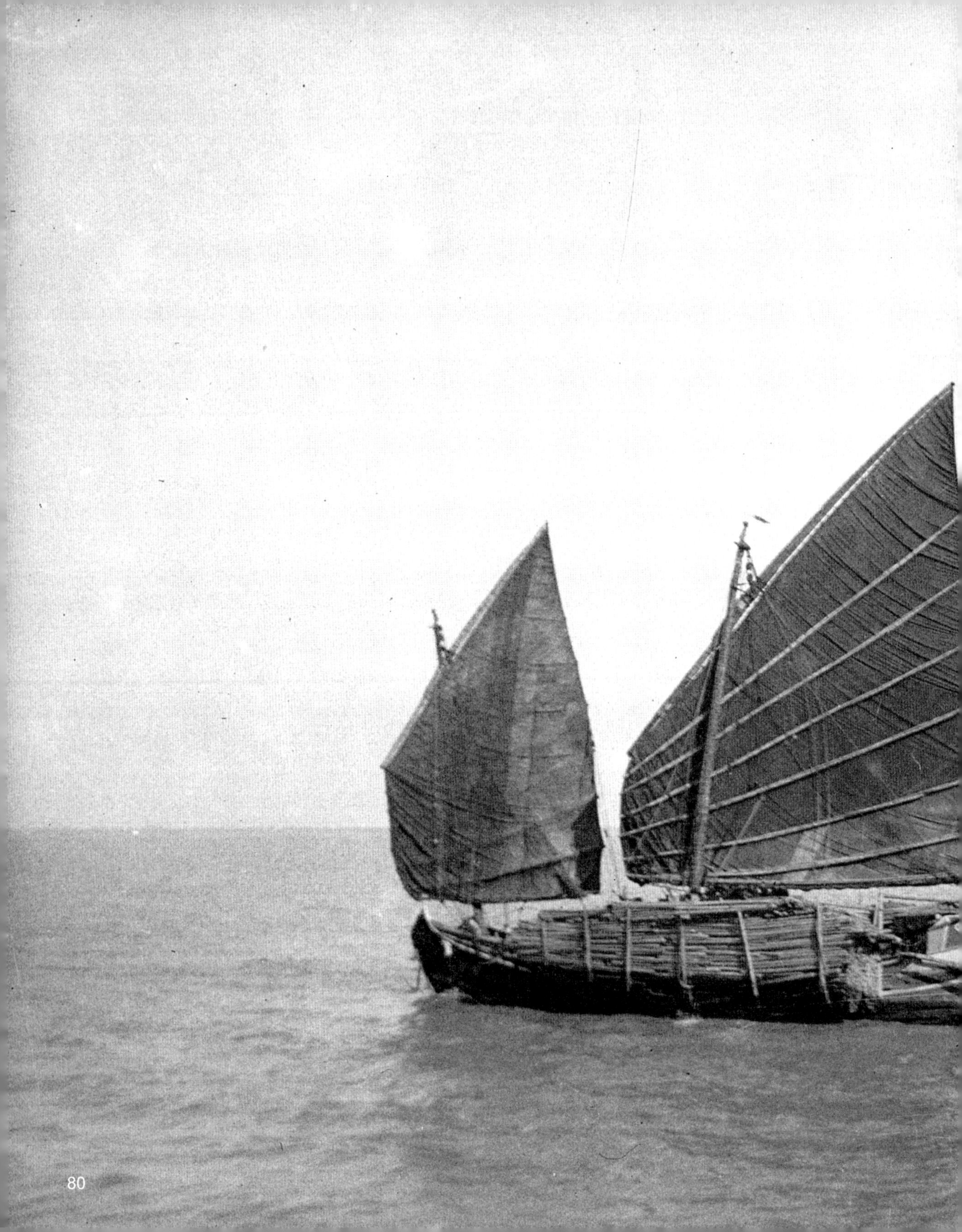

福船-5 | Pole Junk-5

福建三都澳船

福建三都澳船一般长 18~21 米，宽 3.6~4.2 米，通常是三桅帆船，悬挂由棕色帆布制成的斜桁帆，主要运送茶叶。艏艉的甲板为平铺式，舱口略高出甲板平面。船艏为开口式，开口处存放有锚，舷墙向前延伸、向上弯曲、向两外侧倾斜，形成雅致的"两腮"。船艉较宽，船员的住舱就在船艉的甲板室，舱壁后侧的井型座舱可以为舵工和船员遮风挡雨。高高的舷墙贯穿艏艉，可以挡住海水保持船上干燥。

Fujian Sandu Bay Trading Junk

The size of a Sandu Bay trading junk ranged from length of 18~21 metres and beam of 3.6~4.2 metres. Usually there were three masts with sails of canvas, a planked deck continuous from bow-to-stern, with the cargo hatch raised slightly above it, and an open-type bow with the anchors. The Sandu Bay trading junk mainly carried tea. The bulwarks extended forward, curving upward and tilting outwards, forming a pair of elegant "cheeks". There was a wide stern with deck quarters to accommodate the crew. Aft was a well-shaped cockpit providing shelter for helmsmen and crew, and fore-to-aft high bulwarks kept the hull dry in a seaway.

福建三都澳商船 | Fujian Sandu Bay Trading Junk

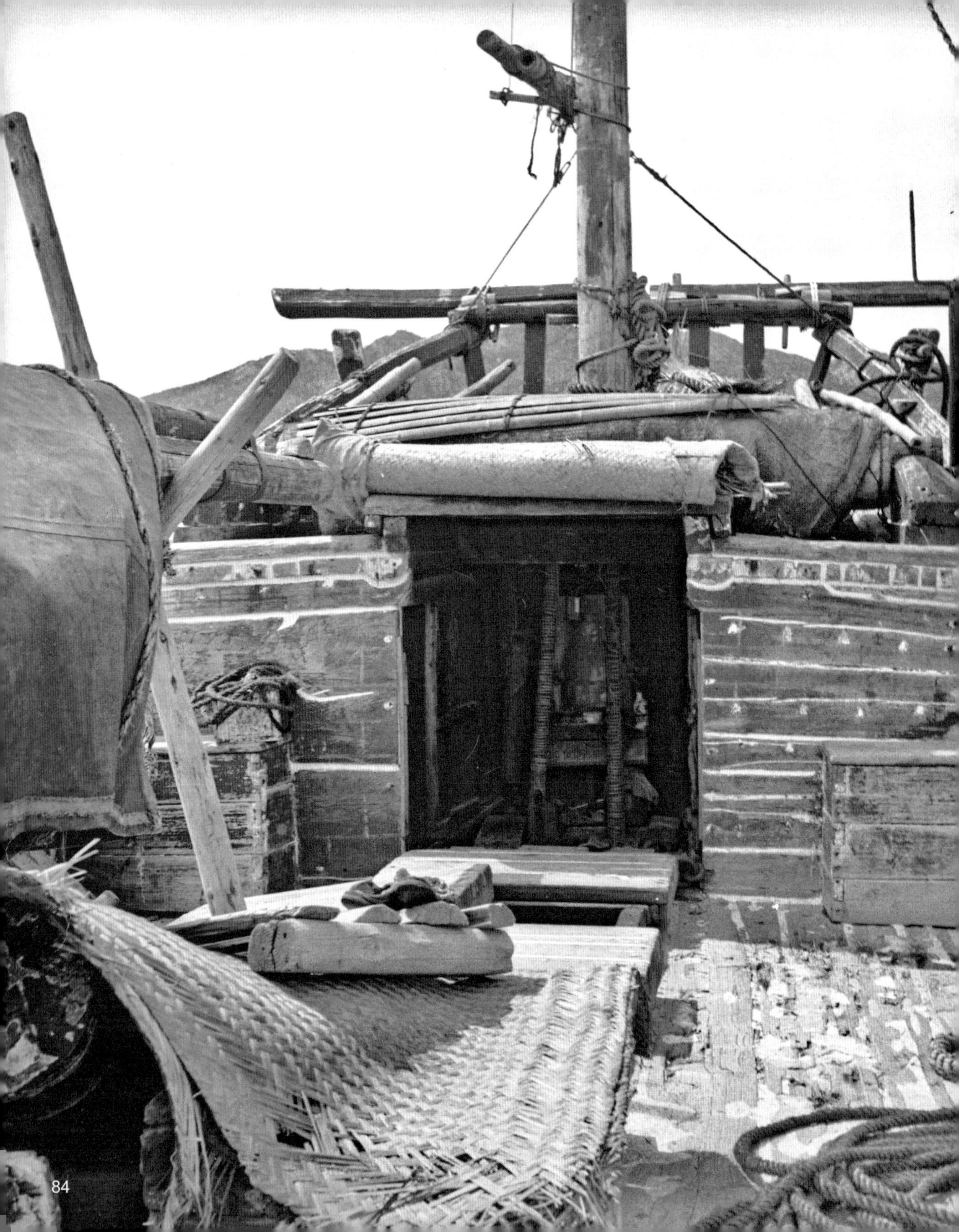

海神妈祖

妈祖，又称天妃、天后、天上圣母，相传为北宋时福建湄洲人，经常拯救海上遇险的船只，为乡亲们行医看病，29 岁时在一次海难中死去。人们为了怀念她在湄洲建庙祭祀。妈祖信仰的发祥地在福建，当时妈祖被作为多功能的神来崇拜，人们认为她能够护佑航海安全和保佑人们免于水旱、疾病、战争之灾。宋宣和五年朝廷赐妈祖庙号，标志着妈祖从民间之神变为官方承认的海神，元世祖忽必烈册封湄洲神女为"护国明著天妃"，确立了妈祖作为海上保护神的独尊地位。每年春秋两季，朝廷都派官员到湄洲祭奠，妈祖的香火从此兴旺起来，信仰范围从福建向南北发展，遍及广东、江浙、楚淮、山东半岛，甚至环太平洋沿岸。

Sea Goddess *Mazu*

Mazu, also known as the Princess of Heaven, the Queen of Heaven and the Mother of Heaven, is believed to have been born in Meizhou, Fujian in the Northern Song Dynasty. She is believed to have rescued vessels from danger at sea, and to have treated sick people. She is said to have died at the age of 29 in a shipwreck. After that, a temple was built in Meizhou to commemorate her. The birthplace of the *Mazu* cult is Fujian, and she is worshipped as a versatile goddess, who is thought to be capable of guarding the seas and protecting people from floods, droughts, disease and wars. Later she got official advocates and is canonized several times. In the fifth year of Xuanhe's rule, the Court conferred a title on *Mazu*, elevating her from a folk sea goddess to an officially admitted one. Furthermore, in 1281CE Kublai Khan canonized this Meizhou goddess with the title of "Hu Guo Ming Zhu Tian Fei" (illuminating Princess of Heaven who protects the nation), confirming her unique status as a sea goddess. Once the *Mazu* temple was flourishing, every spring and autumn, the Court would send officials to Meizhou for memorial purposes. *Mazu*'s worship spread from Fujian throughout Guangdong, Jiangsu, Zhejiang, Chuhuai, and even as far as the Shandong Peninsula, Japan and the Pacific coast.

海神妈祖 | Sea Goddess *Mazu*

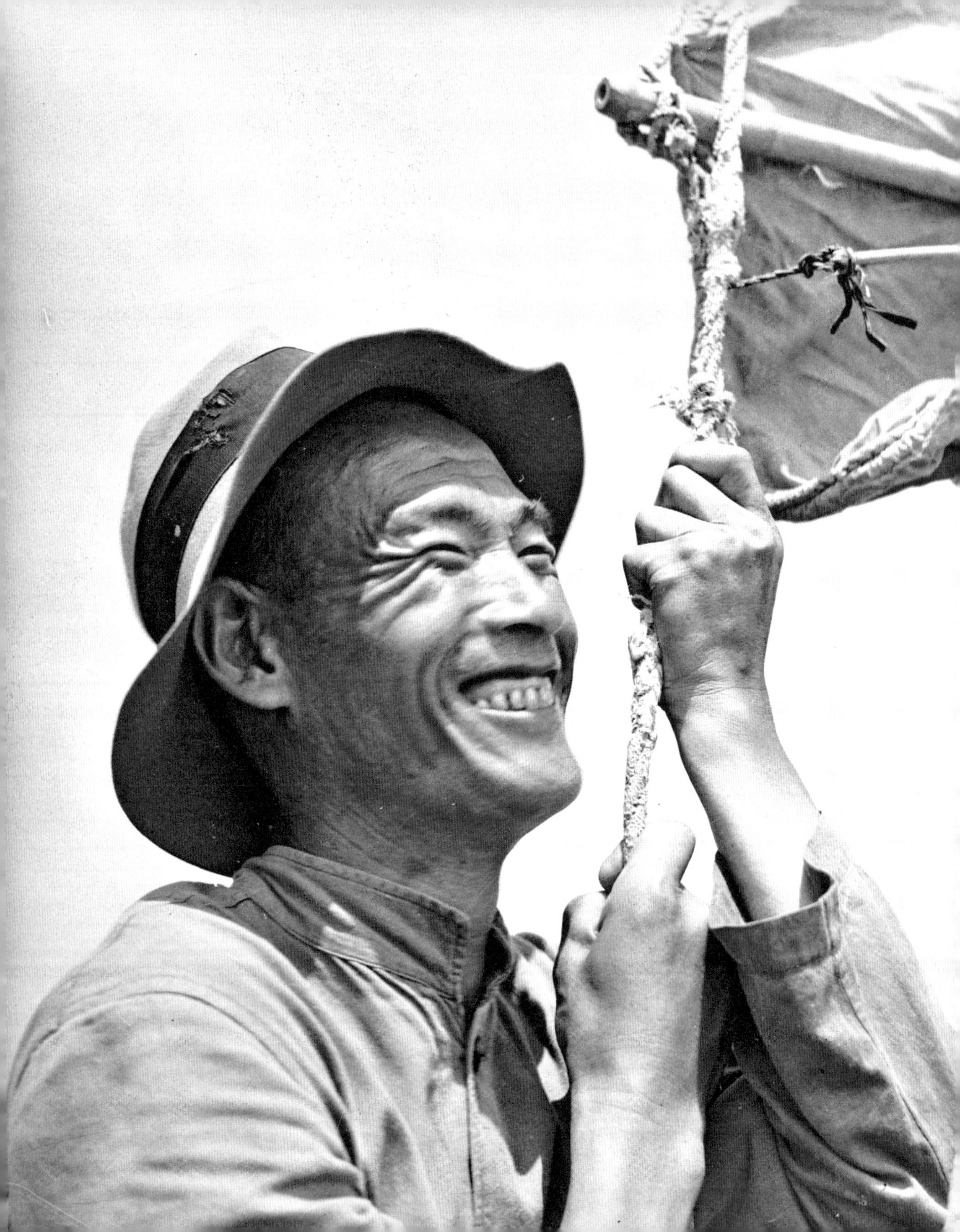

广 东
Guangdong

潮州港 | Chaozhou Port
汕头港 | Shantou (Swatow) Port
广州港 | Guangzhou (Canton) Port
阳江港 | Yangjiang (Yeung Kong) Port

"我们修船也很讲究的，为了讨吉利也要挑良辰吉日，俗话说'搭鱼搭蓬头，修船修缝头'，修船对'缝头'检查特别仔细，船修好后有的也要祭船。"

——广东渔民

"In our region, we paid particular attention to ship repairing, and we usually chose an auspicious date for good luck. As the saying goes 'eat with fish head, repair with boat's roof'. The ship repair must take particular care with the inspection of the seam head. After being repaired, the ship will be sacrificed."

—Fisherman from Guangdong

潮州港 | Chaozhou Port

潮州港

潮州港居我国东南沿海、广东东北部,处拓林湾之中,东临台湾海峡,扼守东海航线和南海航线的交汇要冲,是我国北方和江、浙、闽地区,以及与东南亚、印度洋各国进行海上交往的必经航道。潮州港内风平、浪静、水深、淤积少,是天然良港,其历史可上溯至秦汉,时为当地的造船中心和沿海航运的中继港。明清时期,潮州港是葡萄牙、泰国等国前往漳州的必经之地,与日本也有贸易往来。

Chaozhou Port

Chaozhou Port is situated in the southeast coast of China's mainland and in the northeast of Guangdong Province. It is located in Tuolin Bay with the Taiwan Strait to the east. The port has been a hub of the eastern and southern China Sea routes, and a crucial place for maritime connections between northern China, the Jiangsu, Zhejiang and Fujian areas, and the countries of South-East Asia and the Indian Ocean. Chaozhou is a natural harbour with calm and deep water and less siltation. The history of Chaozhou dates back to the Qin and Han Dynasties, when it initially appeared as a centre for shipbuilding and a terminal for coastal shipping routes. In the Ming and Qing Dynasties Chaozhou was the obligatory port in the route sailing from Portugal and Thailand to Zhangzhou, as well as an important centre for international trades with Japan.

汕头港 | Shantou (Swatow) Port

汕头港

汕头港位于我国东南沿海、广东东北部，扼韩江、榕江、练江之出海口，东临台湾海峡，素有"岭东之门户，华南之要冲"之誉，历来是粤东、闽西、赣南物资的重要集散地和海上门户，也是广东距离台湾最近的港口。1860年，汕头被迫开埠，逐渐取代原先的樟林港成为粤东的门户和海外贸易基地。20世纪30年代，汕头的商业贸易达到鼎盛时期，是中国进出口贸易的重要口岸。抗战爆发后，该港口的运输和对外贸易一落千丈。

Shantou (Swatow) Port

Shantou Port is located in the southeast coast of China, in the northeast of Guangdong Province. It guards the estuary where three rivers—Hanjiang River, Rongjiang River and Lianjiang River converge, with the Taiwan Strait to the east. This strategic location makes the port "the entrance of eastern Fujian Province, and the fortress of southern China". It has long performed as a cargo terminal for distribution and an export gateway for eastern Guangdong, western Fujian and southern Jiangxi. Furthermore, it is Guangdong's closest port to Taiwan. In 1860, Shantou was forced to open up as a commercial port and gradually replaced Zhanglin Port as an important entrance and base for international trade in eastern Guangdong Province. In the 1930s, the commercial activities in Shantou peaked, which made Shantou a vital port for China's import and export trade at that period. Nevertheless, the port transportation and external trade suffered a disastrous decline after the outbreak of the Second World War.

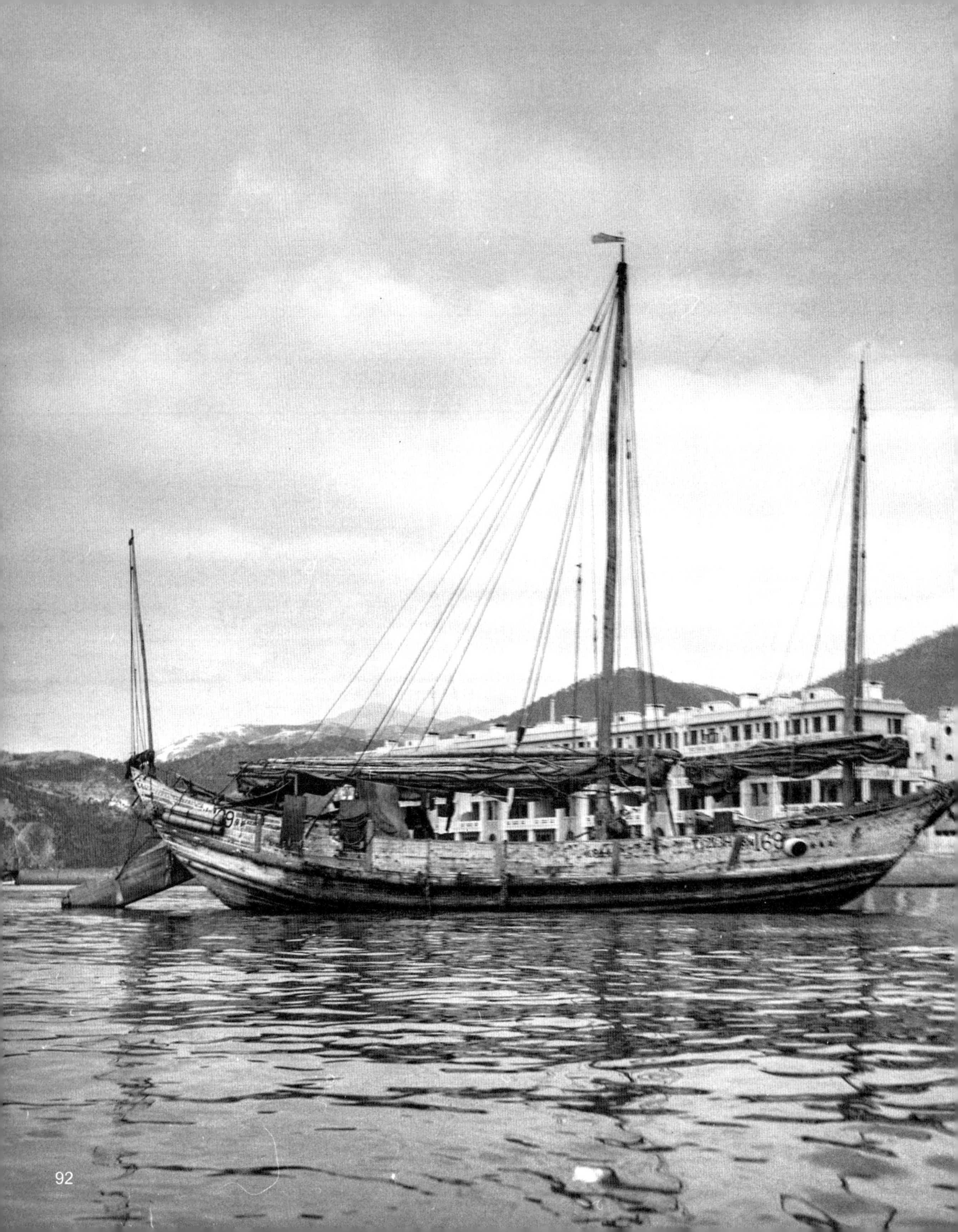
169

汕头渔船-1、2 | Shantou (Swatow) Fishing Junk-1、2

汕头渔船

汕头渔船通常从汕头和韩江口附近的渔村开出,成群结队地作业于汕头港附近的渔场,结束捕捞后驶入港口时,有小舢板出海接应。汕头渔船的特点是:船艏和船艉尖削,船舯宽阔,长9~12米,宽2.4~3米。水线以上的船艏向上前倾,船艉的船艉板为敞开式。该船通常是二桅,偶尔能见到单桅,船帆用棕色布料或帆布制成,下风缘比北方渔船弧度大,竹撑条数量也更多,每一条都用单绑绳和主缭绳连结。从外观上看,渔船前端安有船眼,装饰简朴,船身涂深棕色光漆。

Shantou (Swatow) Fishing Junk

Swatow fishing junks usually sailed from fishing villages near Swatow and the mouth of the Han River, operating in groups in fisheries near Swatow Port. When the evening came they sailed into port, coordinated by small sampans. This type of fishing junk had the following features. It had a narrow bow and stern, with its maximum beam amidships. The length was from 9~12 metres and a beam of 2.4~3 metres. The bow inclined forward above the waterline with a T-shaped stem. There was an open stern transom. The junks were normally two-masted and occasionally single-masted. By the late Qing Dynasty sails were made of brown cloth or canvas. The leech had a much more pronounced roach compared with northern fishing junks and more bamboo battens, each adjusted with single ropes or sheets. Their ship's eye could be observed from ahead. The hull was simply decorated, painted in dark brown with light varnish.

汕头商船

汕头商船应属广船中的艚船类,既能沿海航行,往北可达上海、天津,往南可达海南,也可以出洋远航至东南亚。汕头商船通常建造于粤东地区,有时会具备福船的某些特点,体量比福船稍大,载重约 100~400 吨。这种商船一般会将船头漆成红色,有船眼。原先多以铁力木制造,后来也使用楠木、麻栗木、松木等,用料讲究,结构牢固。其结构特点为:船体上宽下窄,尖底,船型较瘦,舯尖艉宽,两端上翘,甲板脊弧不高,梁拱较小,吃水较深,适合深海航行。采用开孔舵,悬挂扇形撑条式席帆。

Shantou (Swatow) Trading Junk

The Shantou trading junk could be classified as part of the Cao Chuan category of Guangdong junks. It was capable of both coastal sailing, north to Shanghai and Tianjin and south to Hainan, and of overseas voyages to South-East Asia. It was built in eastern Guangdong, so sometimes shared certain characteristics with pole junks, though slightly larger with a deadweight of 100~400 tons. The bow was normally painted red with a ship's eye. The original material used to be nagkassar, before other types of wood such as nanmu or pine were used. It was well-built with good materials. Its structural features included being wide across the deck and narrowing towards the waterline, with a sharp deadrise from the keel and a deep draught. The bow at the cutwater had a fine entry which made it suitable for deep sea navigation. The sheer rose to both bow and stern, but was not pronounced. The deck had little camber, the rudder was fenestrated and the sails had the characteristic large roach of southern junks.

汕头商船 | Shantou (Swatow) Trading Junk

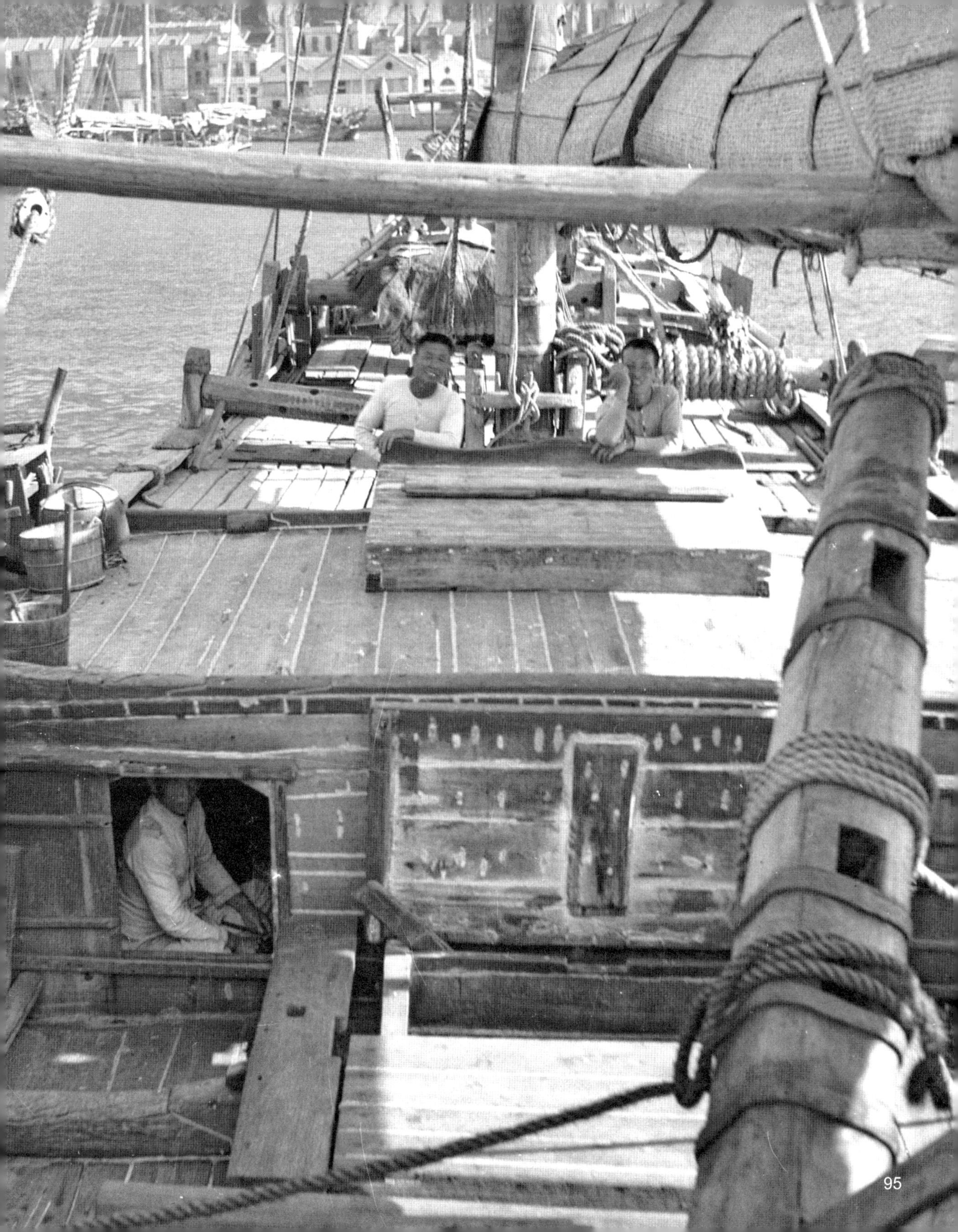

广州港

广州港是我国古代"海上丝绸之路"始发港之一，位于珠江入海口，地处珠江三角洲地区中心地带，濒临南海，毗邻香港、澳门。地理位置优越，港湾优良，具有海、河运输的双重特性。自秦汉时期广州古港形成以来，航船南来北往，沿海运输相当繁忙；同时，其对外贸易历久不衰，是中国与东南亚各国海上贸易的主要港口，也是远航至印度、非洲、欧洲及阿拉伯地区的中转站。1842年,《南京条约》签订后，被辟为五个通商口岸之一。

Guangzhou(Canton) Port

Guangzhou Port was one of the departure ports of the Chinese Ancient "Maritime Silk Road". It sits on the estuary of the Zhujiang River, in the centre of Zhujiang Delta, on the coastal area of the South China Sea and next to Hong Kong and Macao. Guangzhou is a natural harbour with superior location, therefore it served both maritime and inland river transpotation. After its establishment in the Qin and Han Dynasties, the port became a link for China's north-south coastal transportation and a historical major port for international trade between China and conturies in South-East Asia. Moreover, it became vital as a transit station for routes to India, Africa, Europe and Arab region. After the signning of the Treaty of Nanjing in 1842, Guangzhou was opened up as one of the five treaty ports in Qing Dynasty.

广州港 | Guangzhou (Canton) Port

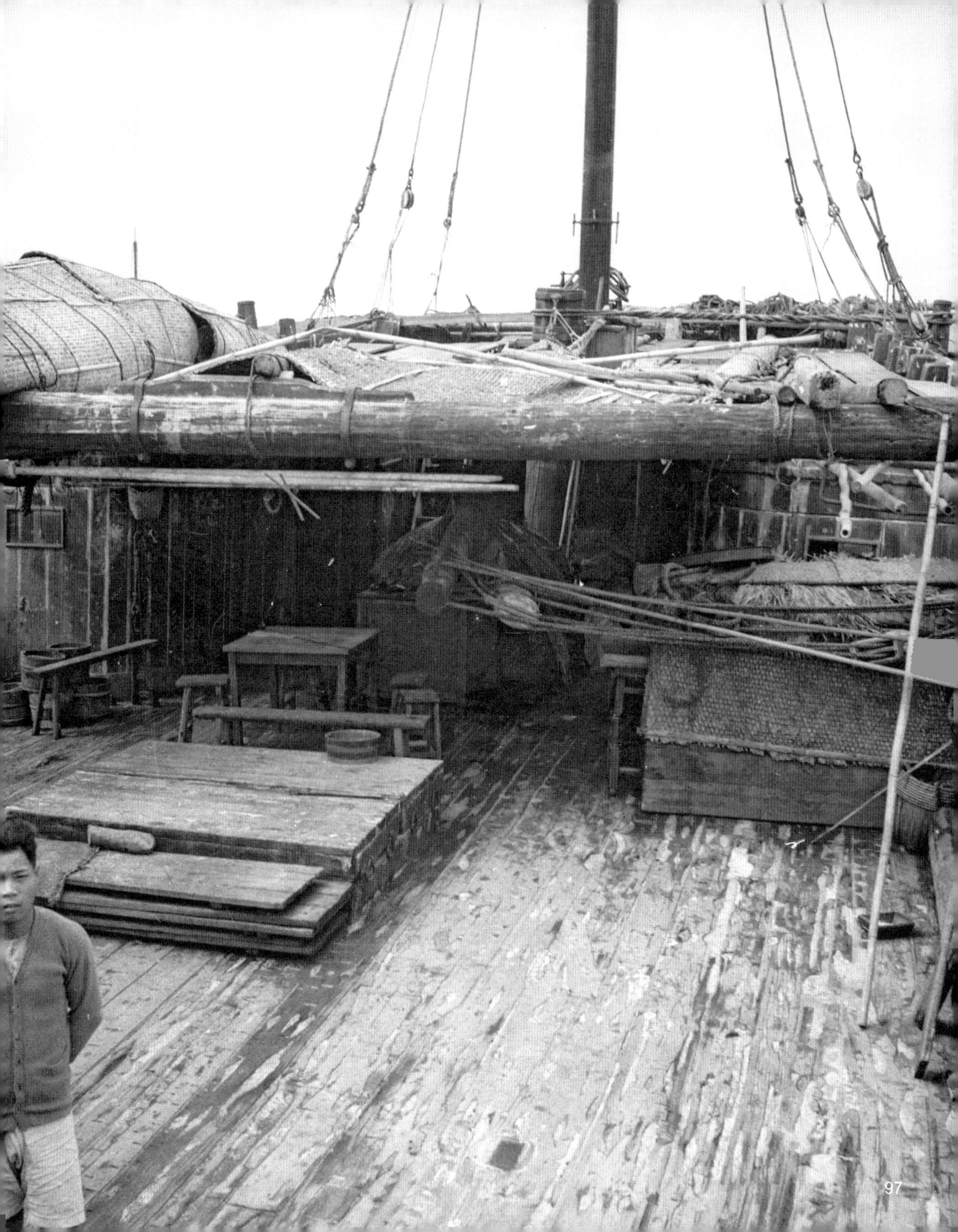

广东盐船-1 | Guangdong Salt Junk-1

广东盐船

该船是运盐到内陆地区的商船。广东盐在明洪武年间便已销到湖广及江西南部地区，运输路线经由广西梧州到平乐府，进入桂林后再载往各地。广东盐船一般不立独桅杆，而是以两根立柱悬帆，船帆用产于闽、广地区的蒲葵制成，不像中原的船帆那样可以转动，因此逆流航行时要靠纤绳牵拉。盐在清代属盐运使司管辖，只能由政府特许的商人承包贩运，贩运时采用引票制，因此广东盐船的船夫水手一般是受制于盐商的专业队伍，领取工食度日。

Guangdong Salt Junk

As the name suggested, the Guangdong salt junk was used to transport salt to inland areas. In the Ming Dynasty, during Hongwu's rule, salt from Guangdong had already been sold to Hubei, Hunan and southern Jiangxi, through shipping routes from Wuzhou, Guangxi to Guilin (Pinglefu) and then other places. The shape and cut of the junk was unique, instead of a single mast, it had a bipod with sails made from palm leaves from either Fujian or Guangdong. They could not rotate like the sails on junks from the central mainland areas, so this junk needed to be pulled via towropes when sailing upstream. In the Qing Dynasty, salt was controlled by the Administrative Office of Salt; it could only be contracted and sold by government-licensed merchants. Therefore, Guangdong boatmen were actually professional teams employed by salt merchants and paid wages.

广东盐船-2 | Guangdong Salt Junk-2

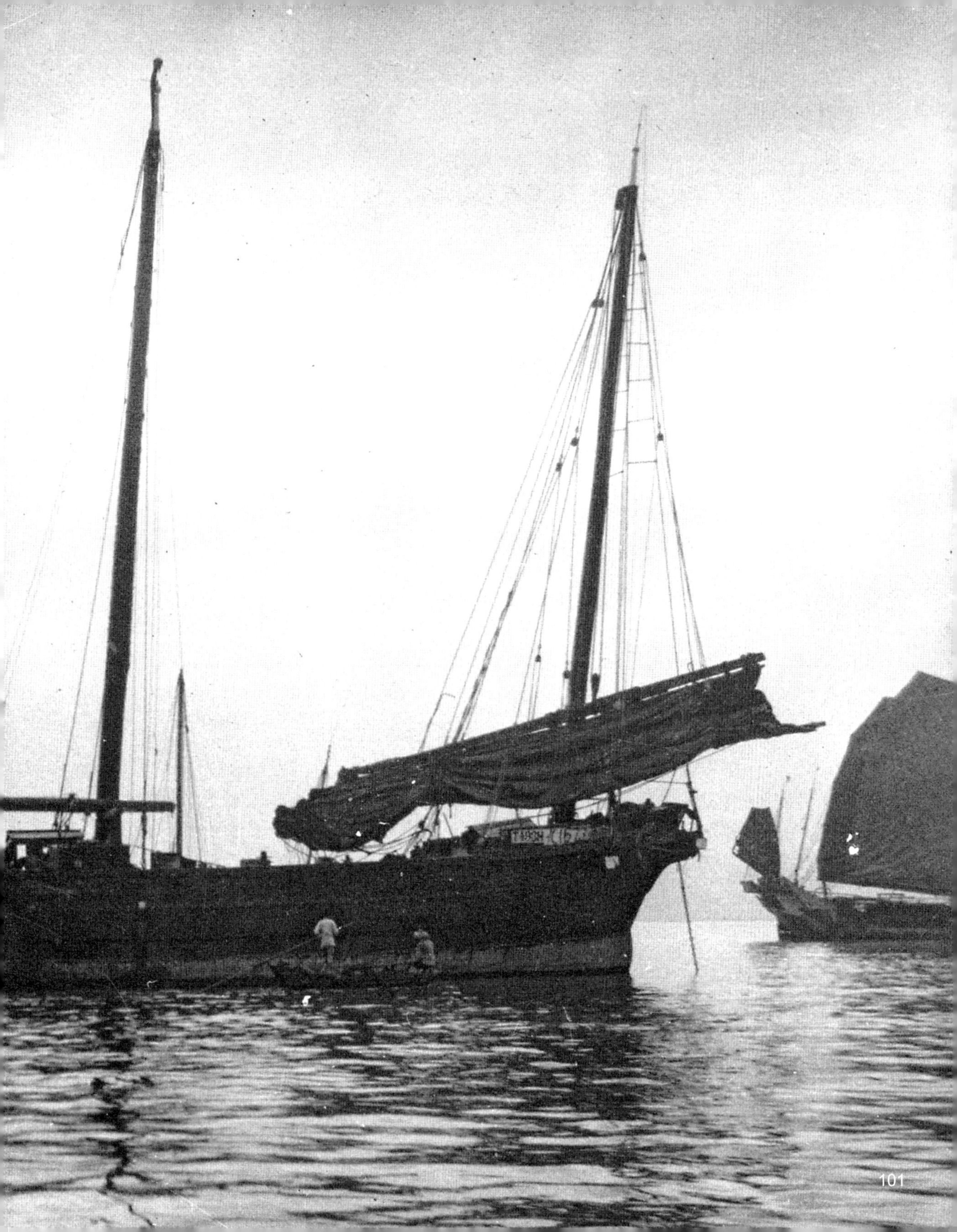

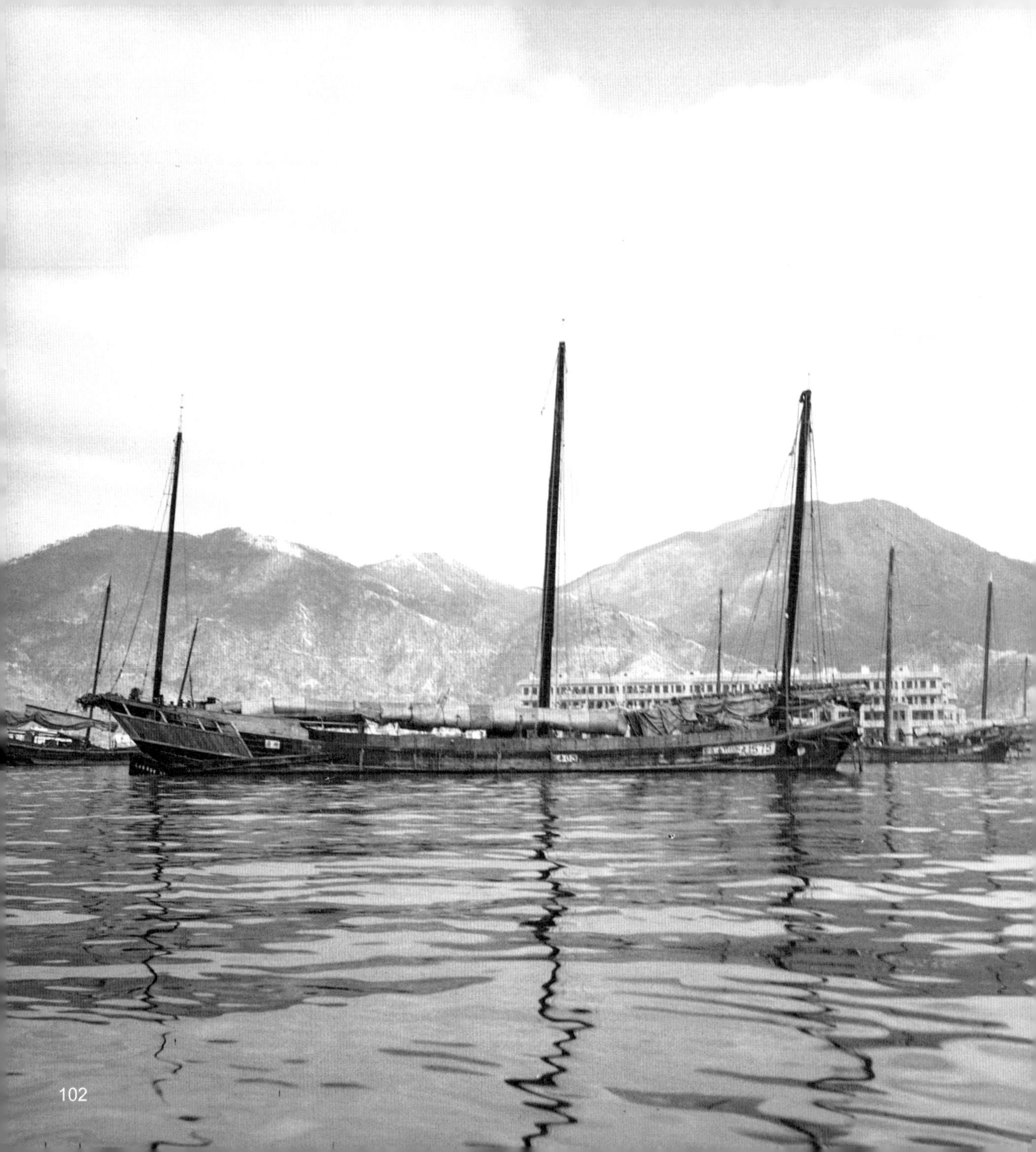

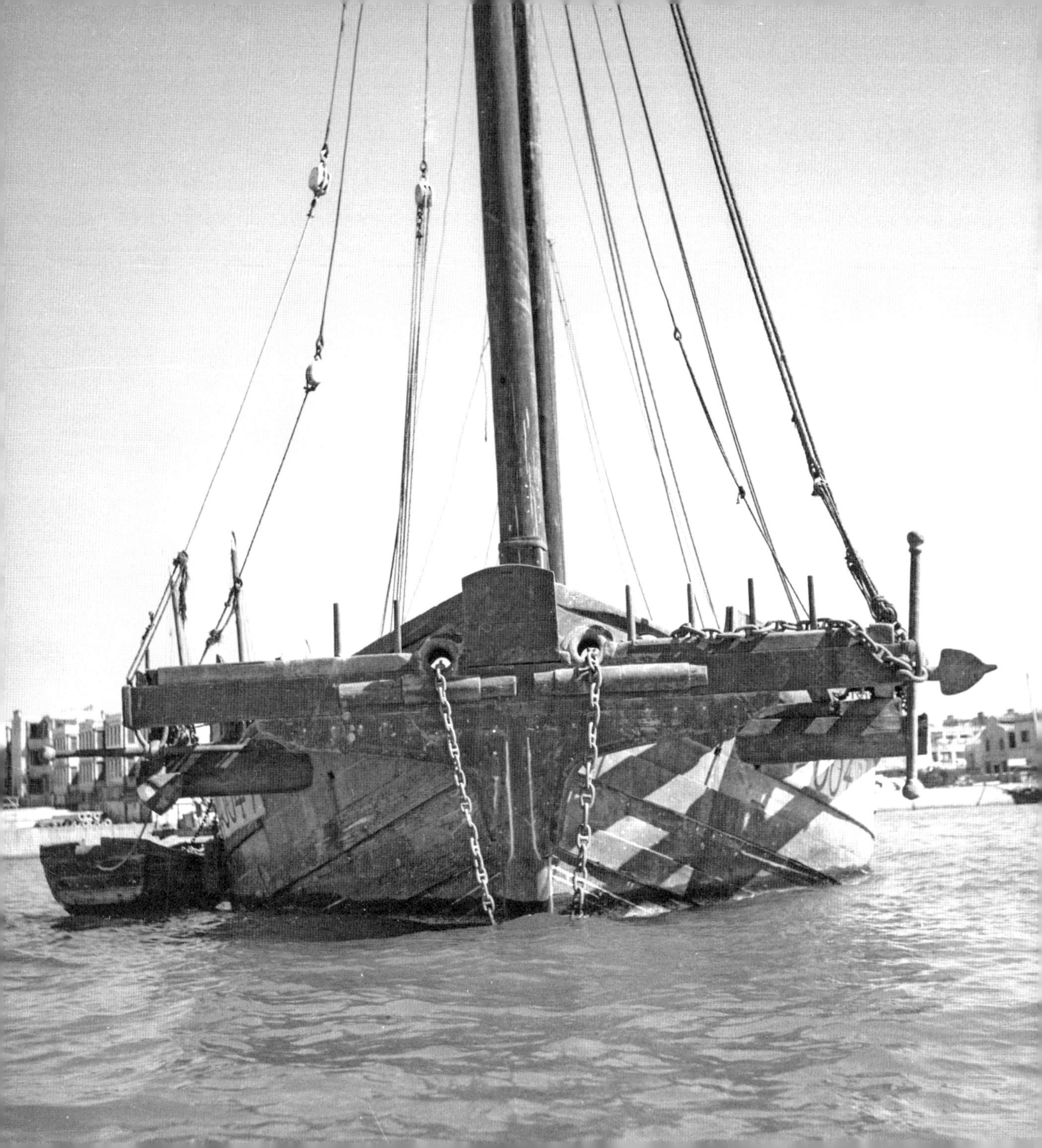

开孔舵-1 | Fenestrated Rudder-1

开孔舵

广船的开孔舵是一种平衡舵，垂直布置，船艉有虚梢（假尾）可以对开孔舵起保护作用。舵叶略呈四方形，展舷比约为 1.0，舵叶上开有许多菱形孔，这样既可以在不影响舵效的情况下大大减小操舵力矩。大型海船为了航行安全，舵一般使用铁犁木这样的优质木料。一艘船上往往有多副舵，还有备用舵。

Fenestrated Rudder

The fenestrated rudder on various types of southern junks was a type of unbalanced rudder. Usually, because the steering systems of traditional junks were vulnerable, junks were equipped with spare rudders. The outboard ratio was 1.0. The diamond-shaped holes significantly reduced the pressure differential between the two sides without greatly affecting efficiency. For the safety of navigation, large seagoing vessels would use a high-quality timber made of nagkassar, for its rudder blade. To enhance steering ability in strong currents, auxiliary rudders were also used in some types of junk.

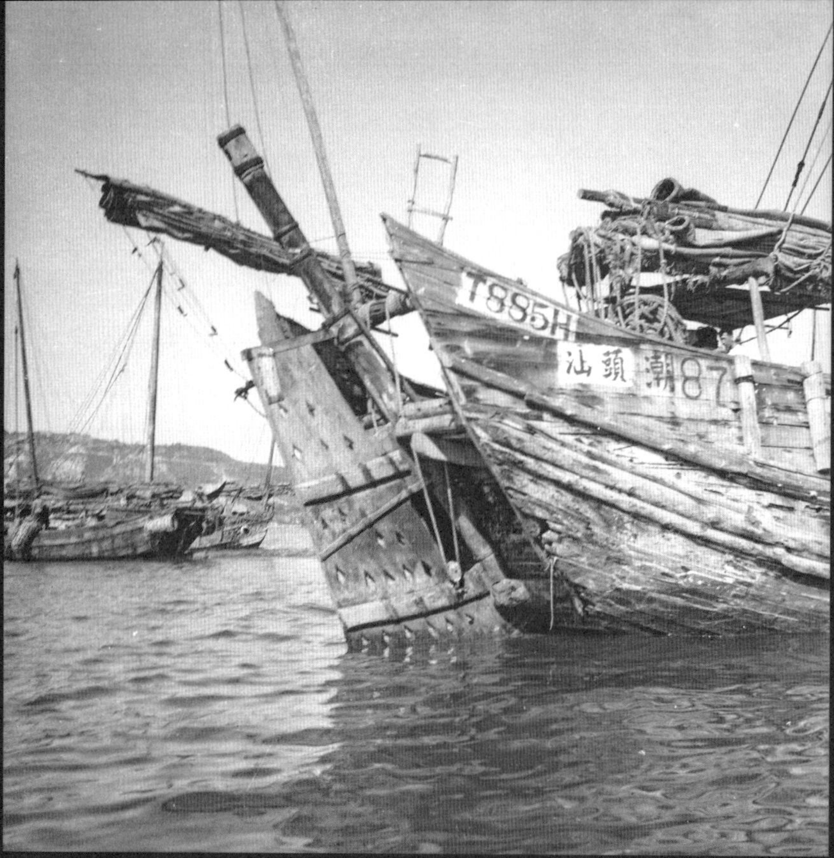
T885H
汕頭
潮87

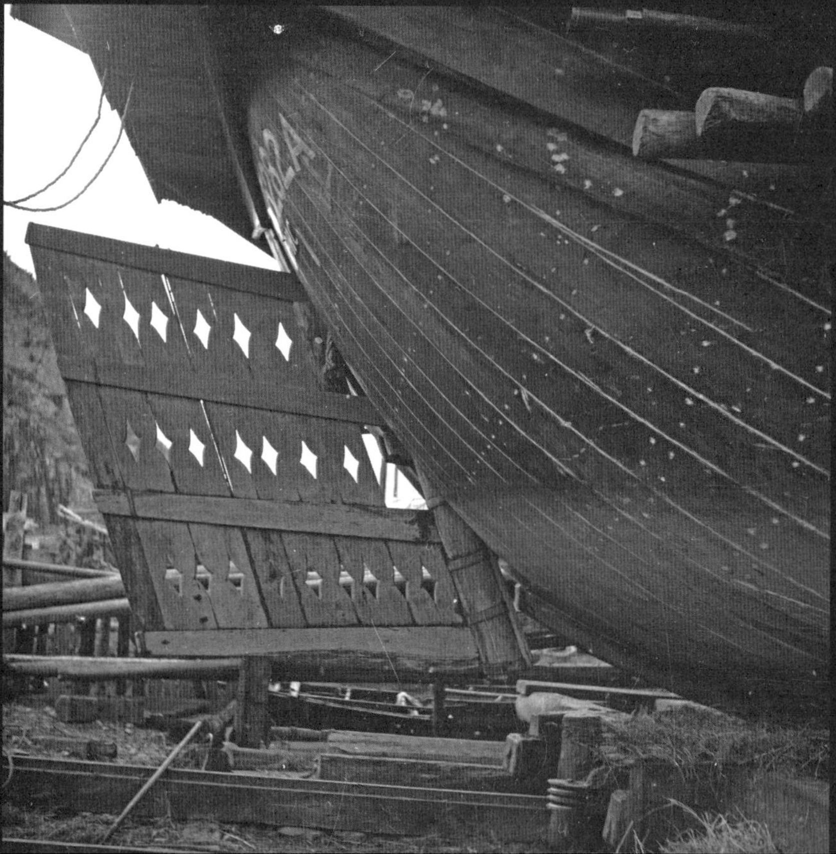

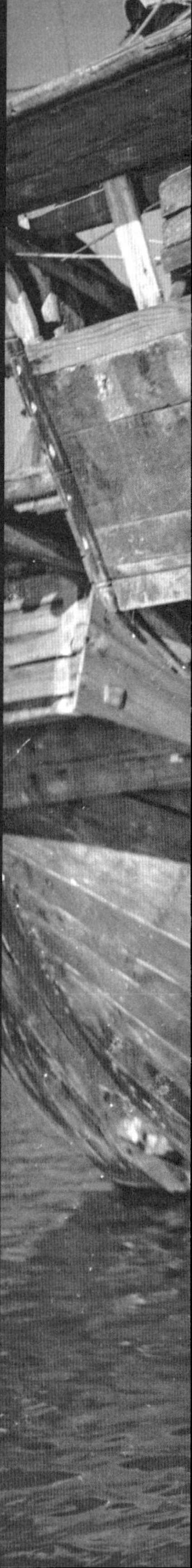

开孔舵-2~4 | Fenestrated Rudder-2~4

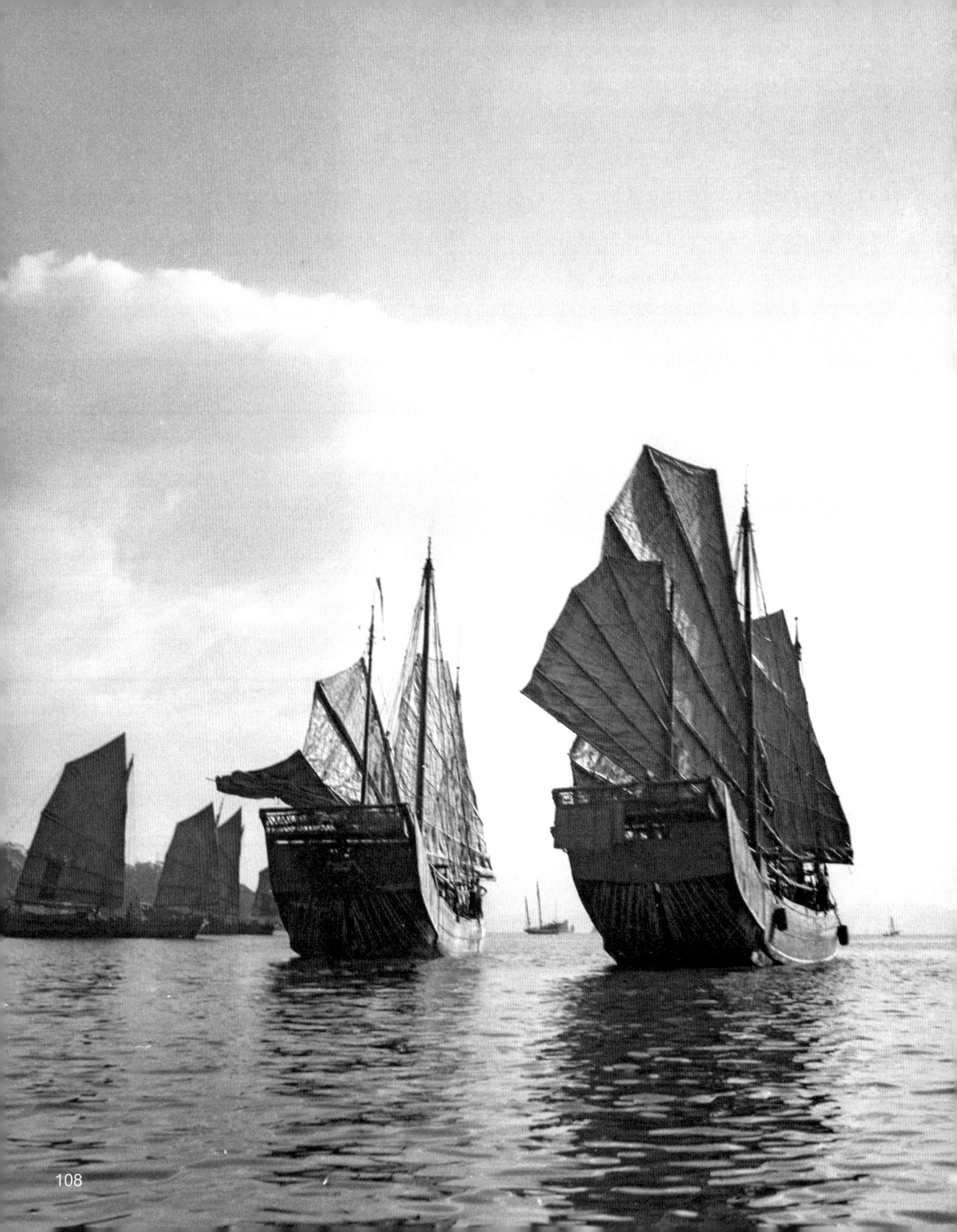

阳江港

阳江港位于广东省阳江市西南约 25 公里的海陵湾,地处广州港和湛江港两大主枢纽港之间,濒临南海,毗邻东南亚各国。凭借良好的地理位置与港湾条件,历史上逐渐成为广东向南海路与珠江三角洲的重要交通咽喉,是商旅集贸港、转运港及重要渔港,通往广州、香港等地商船、渔船多停泊于此。鸦片战争爆发后,随着香港、广州等通商口岸的开放,阳江的对外贸易逐渐衰落。

Yangjiang (Yeung Kong) Port

Yangjiang Port is situated in Hailin Bay, which is 25 kilometres southeast away from Yangjiang City, Guangdong Province. In the middle of the two major pivotal ports, Guangzhou Port and Zhanjiang Port, Yangjiang faces the South China Sea and adjoins the countries in South-East Asia. Benefiting from a favourable geographic location and natural harbour conditions, the port gradually became the strategic hub of the Zhujiang Delta and southward shipping route from Guangdong. Berthing most of the commercial and fishing junks sailing to Guangzhou Province and Hong Kong Yangjiang was multifunctional as a trade port, an entrepot and an important fishing port. After the outbreak of the Opium War, with the rising of treaty ports such as Hong Kong and Guangzhou, the export trade of Yangjiang Port decreased.

阳江港 | Yangjiang (Yeung Kong) Port

七艕

七艕是在阳江建造的是一种拖网渔船，通常船长 22 米，宽 4.5 米，深 1.6 米，三桅。"七艕"是广东地区典型的船型，结构坚固，船型狭长，尾部有较高的上层建筑，航行稳定性好，行动敏捷，操作灵活，采用插板和升降开孔舵。插板，舵，前后帆可联合操纵。船帆呈大折扇形，像蝴蝶的翅膀，很具特色。

Seven Pang (Qi Pang)

Seven Pang was a traditional three-masted junk which was built in the Yeung Kong area. It was usually 22 metres in length, 4.5 metres in beam and 1.6 metres in depth. Its stern was a typical trawler in the Guangdong area, with its bow sharp at the cutwater. Its appearance was very unique with its stern rounded up, ending in a high and wide transom, a fenestrated rudder hanging below the bottom, and a foldable fan-shaped sail that looked like butterfly wings.

七艕-1 | Seven Pang (Qi Pang) -1

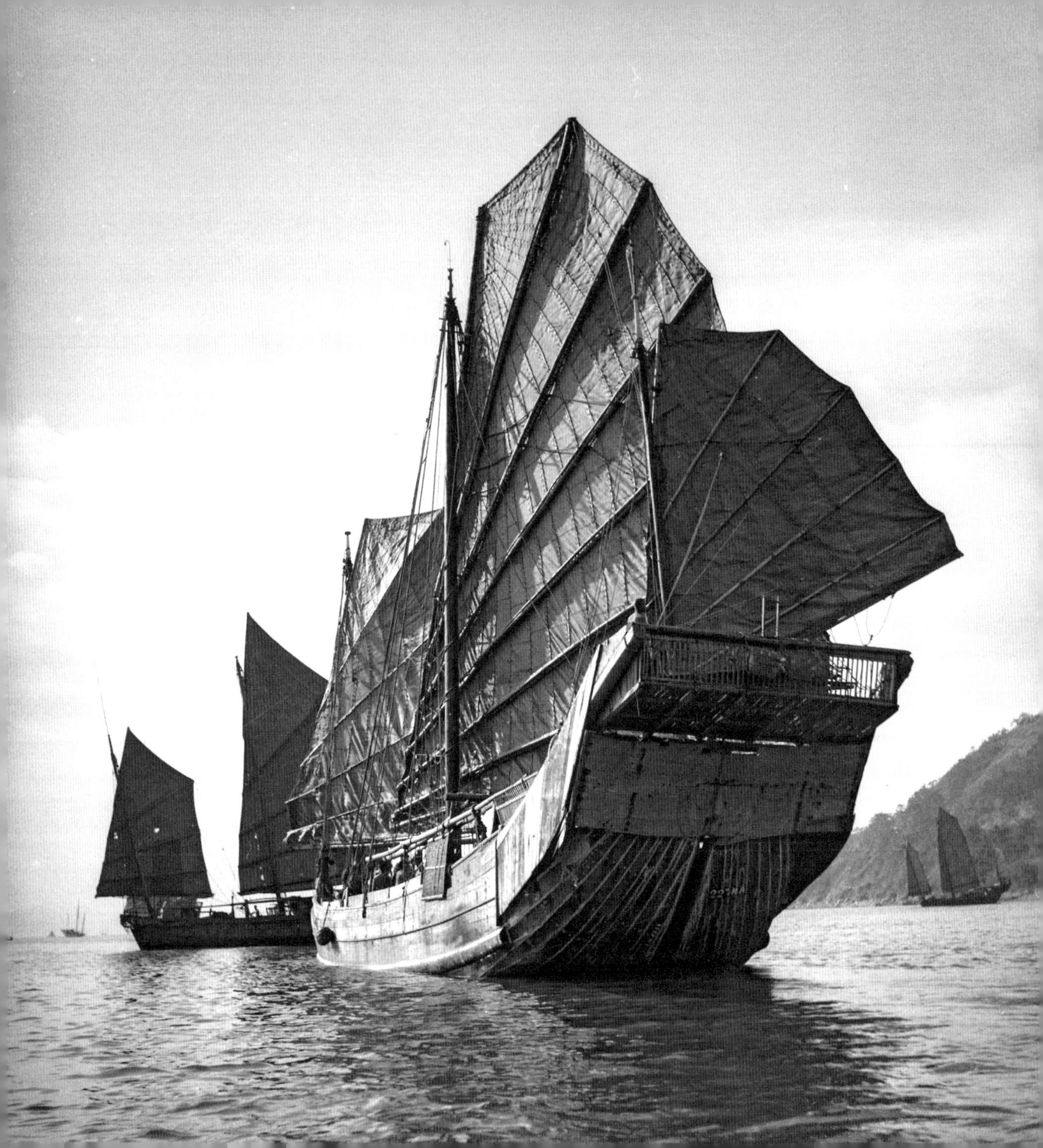

113

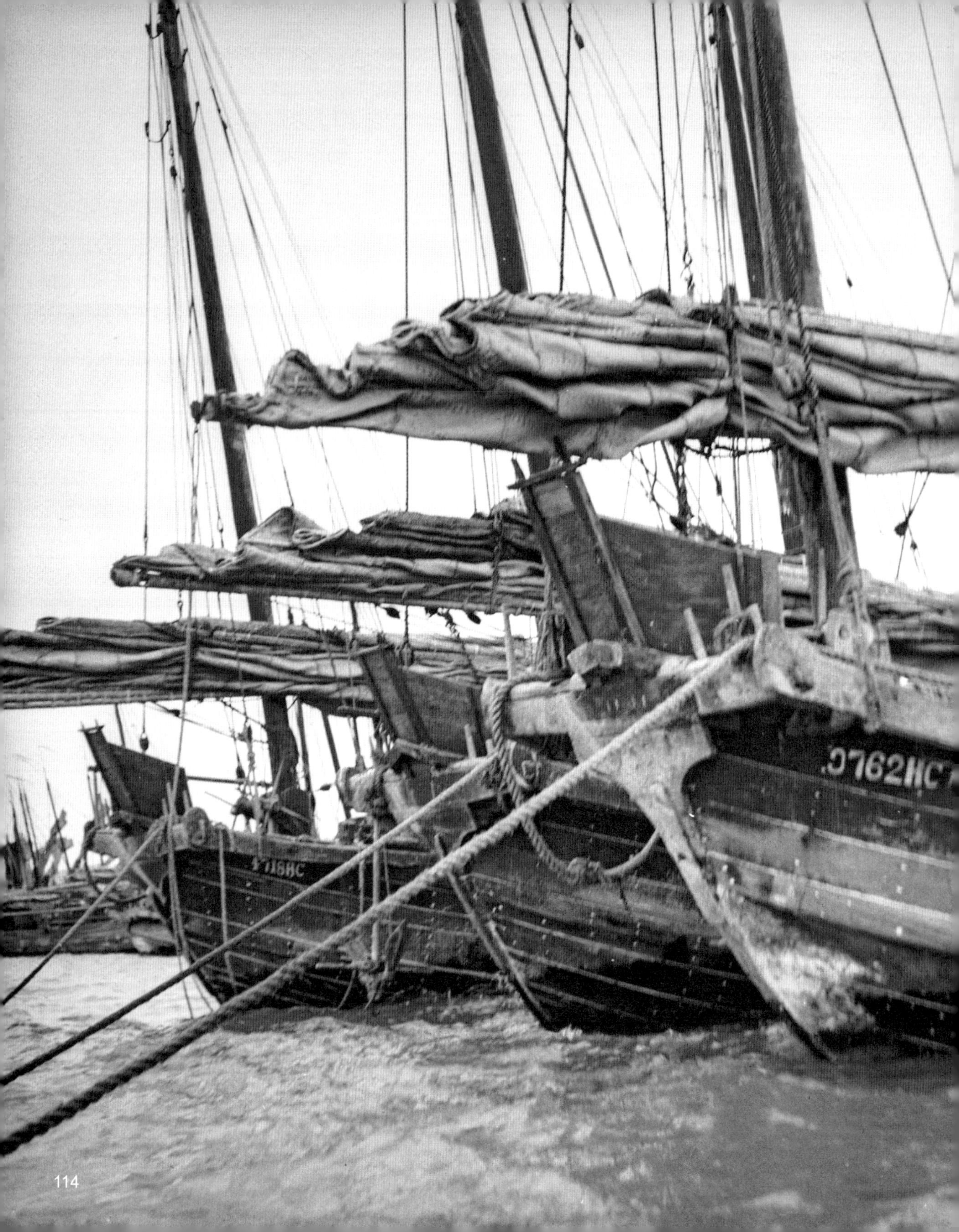

海南商船

海南商船频繁往返于海南岛和东南亚各国之间，有时也作为捕鱼船使用。船长 25.6 米，宽 5.5 米，船深 1.6 米，通常船上有 16~20 名船员。船艏尖削，悬挂铁锚，船舯到船舯比较平直，船艉高耸而起，采用升降开孔舵，可调节深浅高低。船体拥有主龙骨，配有横插板。船尾吊有小舢板。通常立 3 桅，艏桅前倾，主桅在船中部。它是一种吃水较深、适合深海航行的帆船。

Hainan Trading Junk

The Hainan trading junk traded widely in South East Asia, but also engaged in fishing. It had a length of 25.6 metres, a beam of 5.5 metres, a depth of 1.6 metres and usually 16~20 crew members. With a raked bow, and sharp at the cutwater, its framework projected forward from abreast the foremast and connected across the bow to hold the anchor and running rigging. Its stern rounded up, ending in a high and wide transom; the gallery ran along the quarters and stern; and it had a straight keel. A fenestrated rudder hung below the bottom; the tiller controlled by ropes and blocks; and many had centreboards. The deck had a long hatch amidships, and there were cabins on either side of the rudder head and tiller. A sampan hung from the aft davits. It had three masts with the foremast stepped in the bow, raking forward and the mainmast roughly amidships. It had a deep draught and was suitable for deep sea navigation.

海南商船-1 | Hainan Trading Junk-1

海南商船-2~4
Hainan Trading Junk-2~4

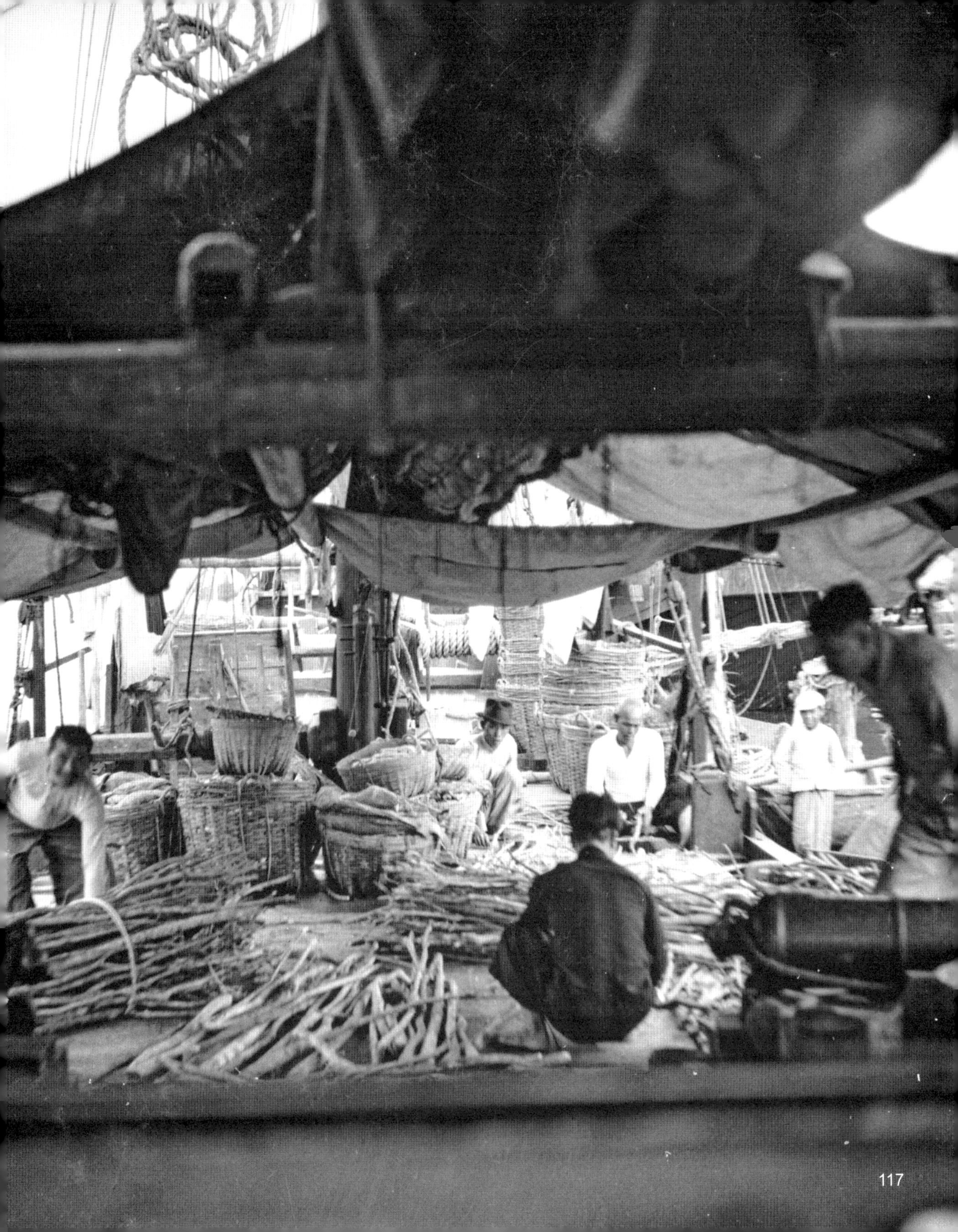

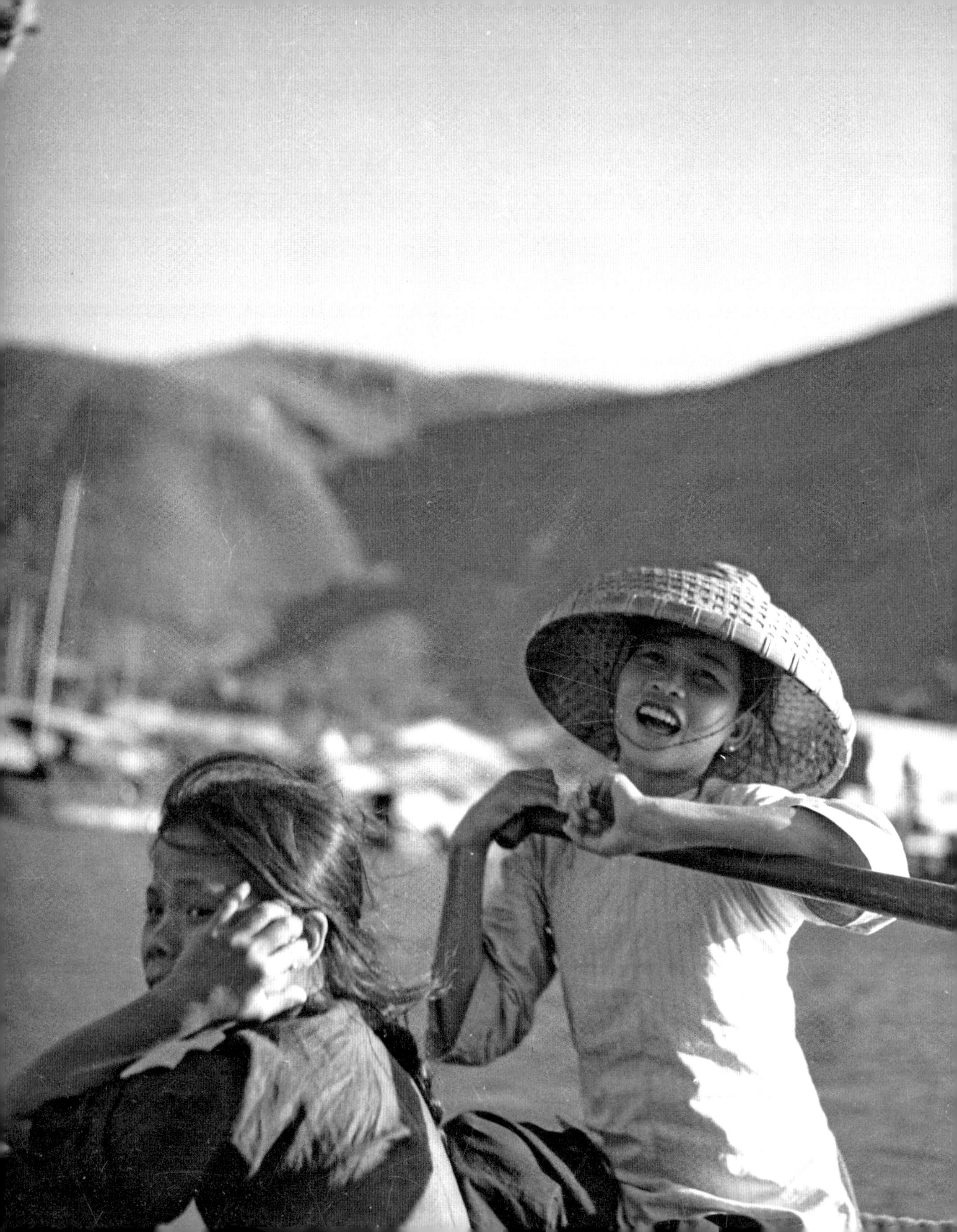

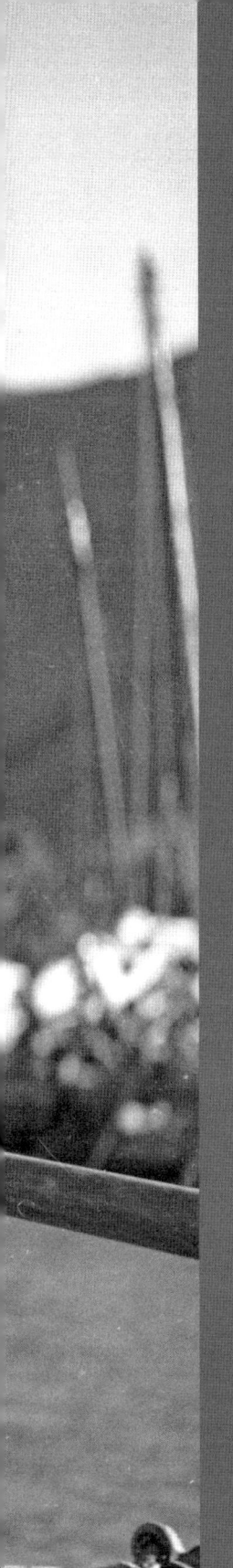

香　港
Hong Kong

香港港 | Hong Kong Port
筲箕湾 | Shau Kei Wan
香港仔 | Aberdeen
吐露港 | Tolo Harbour

"我们当地叫'走船跑马三分命',我们的丈夫经常出海捕鱼,在出海之前首先要祭祀海神妈祖,祈求出海平安。造船的人会在龙骨节点的位置放上七个铜板和一个铜镜,寓意'七星伴月',祈求出海平安。"

——香港渔民

"we used to say that 'sailing or driving horses could cost one's life'. My husband often goes out for fishing, and we usually worship the goddess of sea, *Mazu*, and pray for the peace on board. Shipbuilder usually position seven coins and one bronze mirror on the keel joint, which means 'accompany by the big dipper and moon in the sea', to pray for safe sailing."

—Fisherwoman from Hong Kong

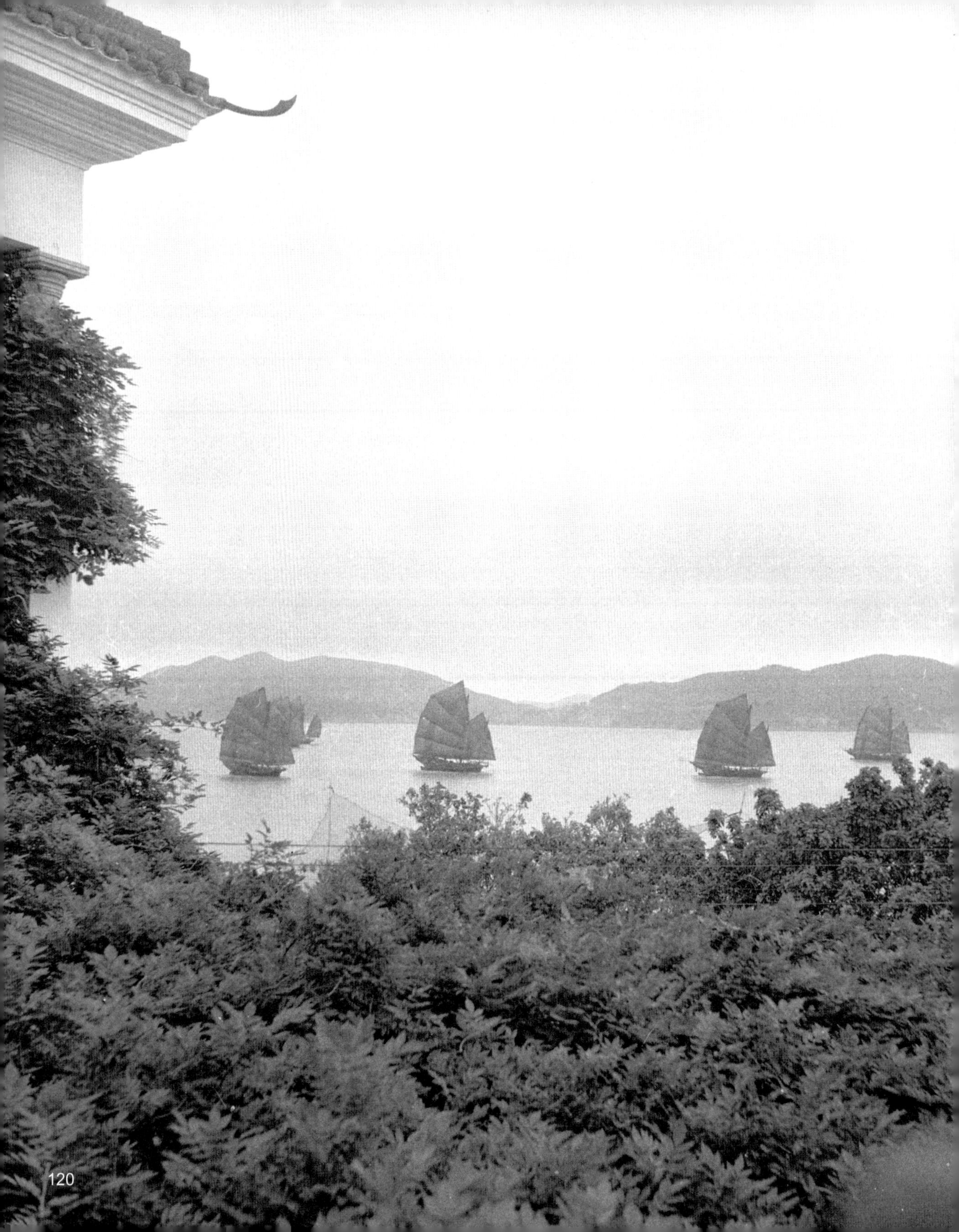

香港港

香港位于中国南海的北岸，珠江三角洲的东岸。港内水深风静，是一个天然良港，便于停靠海船、发展航运。自香港沦为英国的殖民地后，该地成为英国在远东倾销产品的商业基地和进行转口贸易的中心。在近海航线方面，香港与广州、澳门之间有三角航线。位于香港马湾岛和大屿山东北角相接的汲水门海峡，是香港通广州、澳门航运的要津。近海航线也可达汕头、海口、北海等地。由于香港港口建设的发展和转口贸易的兴起，外国到中国进行贸易的远洋轮船都不再直接进出广州港，而是先到香港卸货，再由广州港转运到广州、上海等沿海各通商口岸，中国沿海各通商口岸的货物也主要经由香港输出。

Hong Kong Port

Hong Kong is located in the north coast of the South China Sea, on the east side of the Pearl River Delta mouth. It is a natural fine harbour, deep and quiet. After Hong Kong became a British colony, it soon turned into a depot, a commercial base, and an intermediary trade centre in the Far East for the Great Britain. Hong Kong opened a triangular coastal route from Guangzhou to Macau. Kap Shui Mun Channel, connecting Ma Wan and the northeast corner of Lantau Island, served as a crucial area for shipping between Hong Kong, Guangzhou and Macau. Routes also extended to trading ports like Swatow, Haikou and Beihai. Due to the development of Hong Kong and the rise of intermediary trade, foreign ocean-going vessels to China no longer accessed Guangzhou Port directly, instead, they unloaded the cargoes in Hong Kong first, before the goods were transshipped to coastal trading ports like Guangzhou and Shanghai. Meanwhile, goods from other coastal ports in China were also exported from Hong Kong.

香港港-1 | Hong Kong Port-1

香港-2 | Hong Kong-2

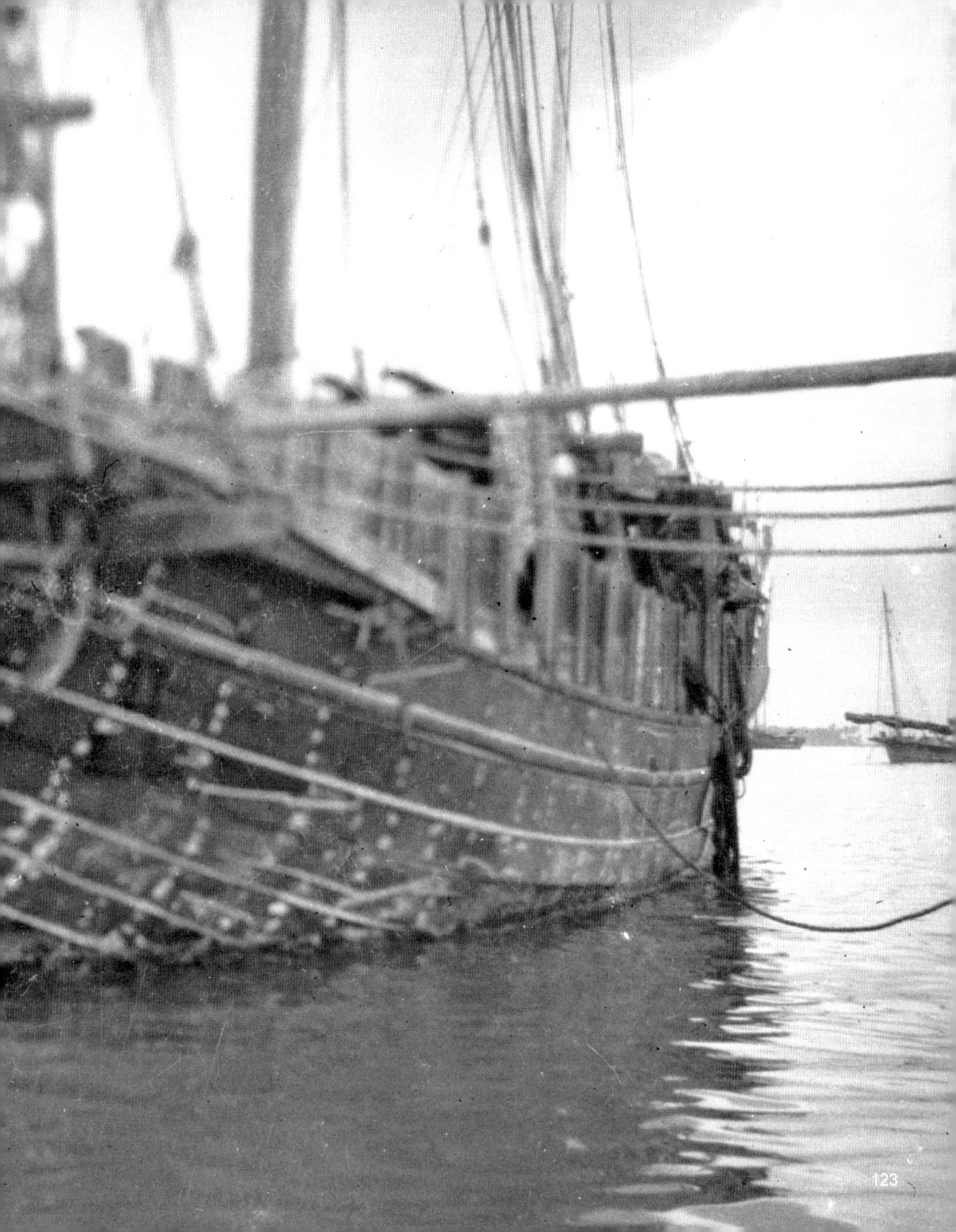

筲箕湾

筲箕湾位于香港岛北部东端，西接鲗鱼涌，南接连柴湾，北接鲤鱼门。该地因其港湾形状像筲箕而得名。港湾不大，但东南边有山做屏障，正好挡住来自太平洋上的东南风。早在 18 世纪，当地渔民就发现这里适宜渔船停泊，来自柴湾的渔民和惠州的客家人开始在这里居住。英国占领香港前，此地已有居民二百余户，1841 年时该地又增至一千余人，是当时岛上最大的市镇之一，后逐渐发展成为水产交易中心。

Shau Kei Wan

Shau Kei Wan was located in the northeast of Hong Kong Island, west of Quarry Bay, north of Chai Wan, on the west of Lei Yue Mun. The name was derived from the shape of harbour, which resembled a Shau Kei (rice washing basket). It was not large in area, but it was sheltered by mountains from the southeast side, which gave protection from the southeast winds of the Pacific Ocean. As early as the 18th century, local fishermen found this place a suitable haven, so fishermen from Chai Wan and Hakka people from Huizhou, working as quarrymen, started to live here. Before the colonial age, there were more than 200 inhabitants; later in 1841, this number increased to more than 1000, making Shau Kei Wan one of the largest villages on the island at that time. After that, it gradually developed to become a major fishing and fish product trading centre.

筲箕湾 | Shau Kei Wan

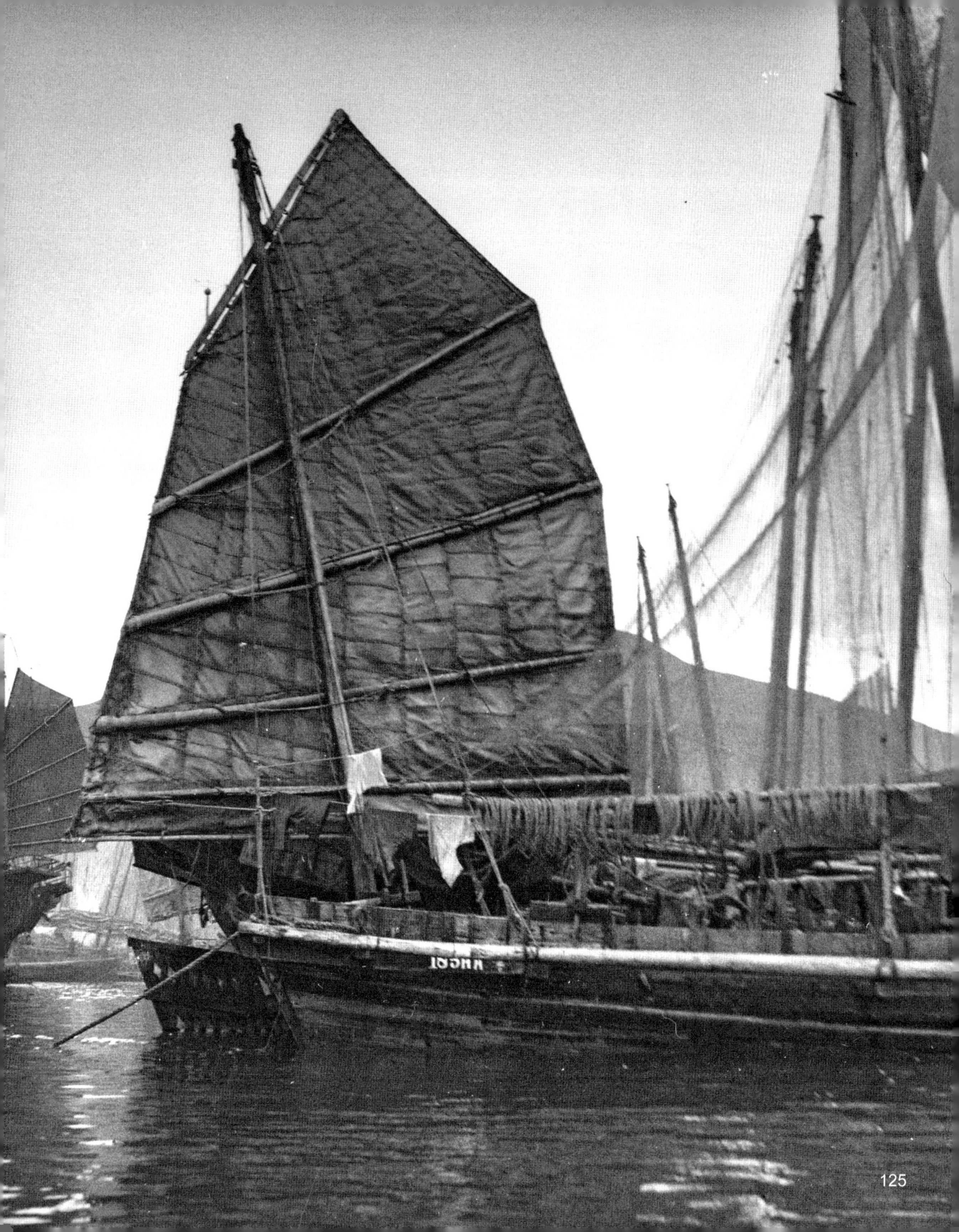

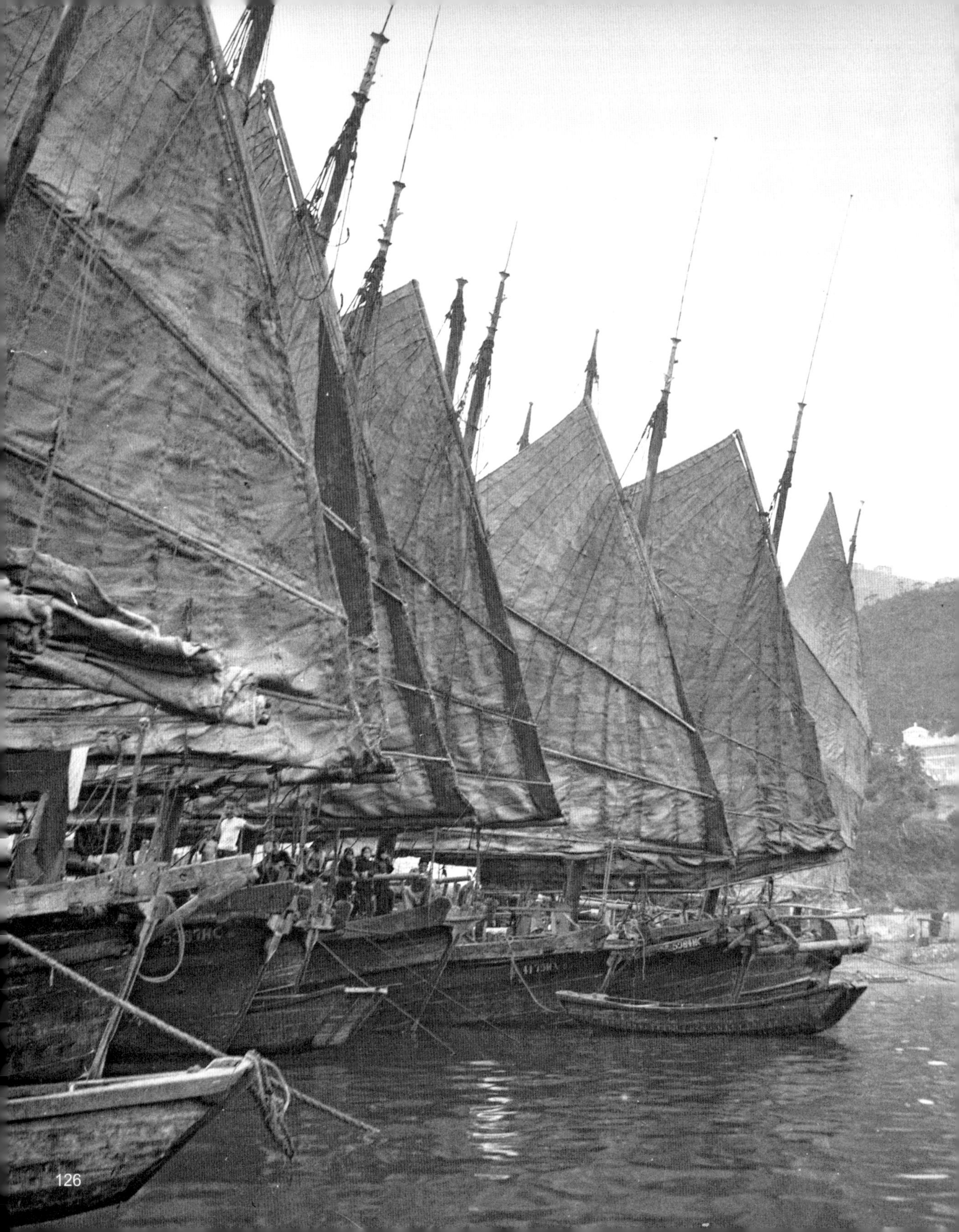

香港仔

香港仔位于港岛南区西部，因岸边多礁石，故又名石排湾，西接华富，东连黄竹坑，南与鸭脷洲相连。香港仔原是一座历史悠久的渔村，曾经是海上运输、船只补给的小港口，因集散莞香得名。香港仔东北面是一片山岭，可阻挡来自东北方向的季候风，西南面又有鸭脷洲岛作为屏障，港湾内可容纳一千余艘渔船停泊，因此成为香港最大的渔港。

Aberdeen

Aberdeen is located in the western part of southern Hong Kong Island. It is also known as Shek Pai Wan due to its rocks. It is connected wih Wong Chuk Hang in the east, Huafu in the west and Ap Lei Chau in the south. Aberdeen had a long history, and was a small port for maritime transport and vessel supply. It became famous because of the distribution of wood from the incense tree (Aquilaria Sinensis). On the northeast of Aberdeen were mountains, which blocked monsoon coming from the same direction; it also enjoyed the shelter of Ap Lei Chau Island from the southwest. The harbour could accommodate more than 1000 fishing junks, and this advantage made it Hong Kong's largest fishing port.

香港仔-1 | Aberdeen-1

香港仔-2、3 | Aberdeen-2、3

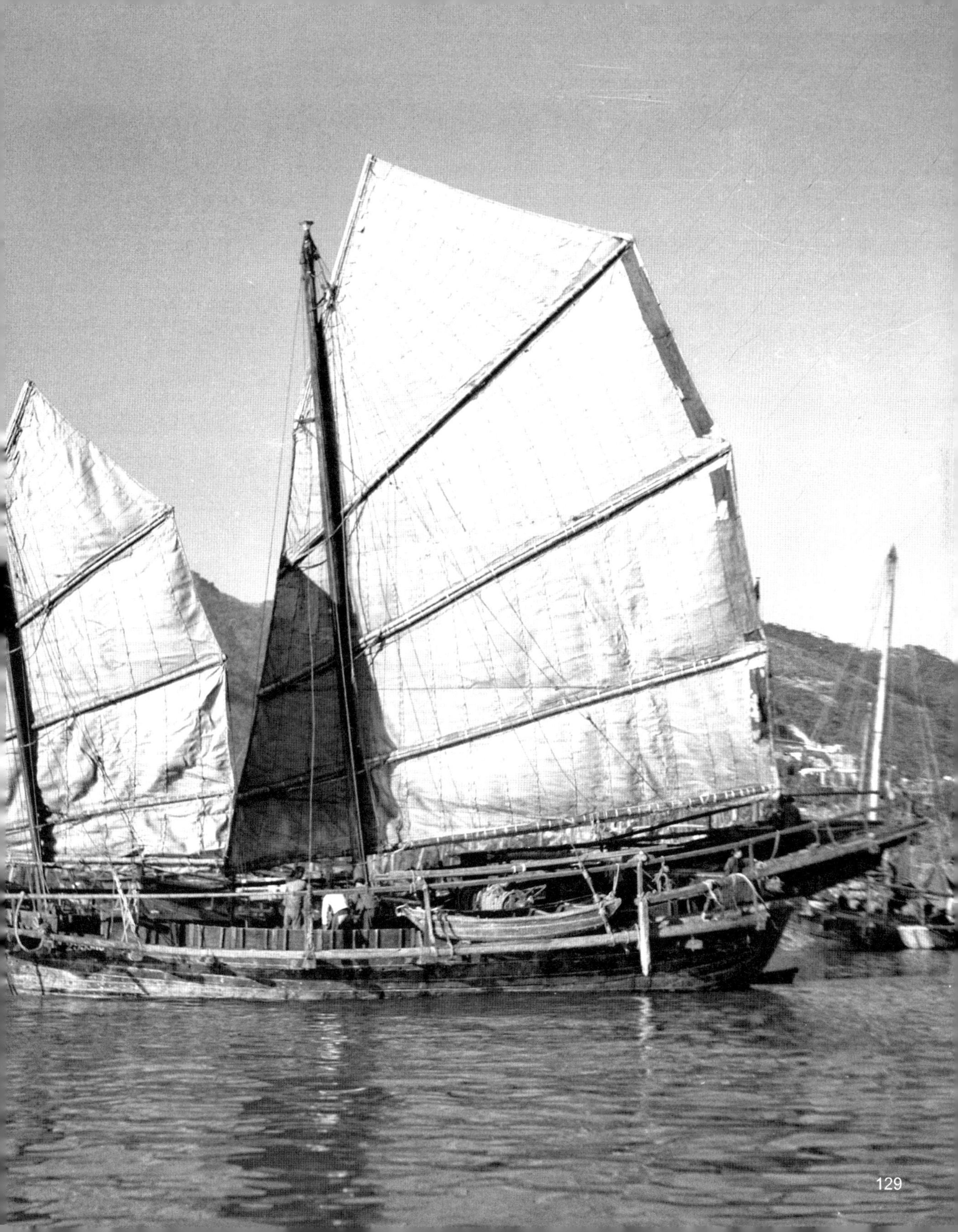

130

吐露港

吐露港，原称大埔海，古称大步海，是香港新界的主要内港之一。大埔海因濒临大埔墟而得名，位于新界东部，北、西、南三面被陆地环抱，仅东北部经窄长的赤门海峡与外海相连。大埔海风平浪静，是著名的海产区和海鱼养殖区。

Tolo Harbour

Tolo Harbour, formerly known as Tai Po Hoi or Tai Po Sea, was one of the main harbours in the New Territories of Hong Kong. Its name was derived from the main settlement of Tai Po Market nearby. Located in the east of New Territories, it is surrounded by land to the north, west and south and only is connected to the sea through the long and narrow waterway now known as Tolo Channel. Tai Po Hoi was quiet without strong winds, and famous for its marine products and mariculture.

吐露港-1 | Tolo Harbour-1

吐露港-2-4 | Tolo Harbour-2-4

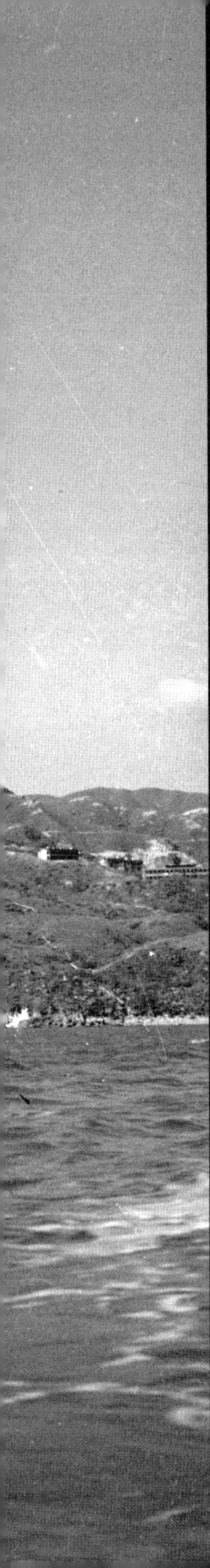
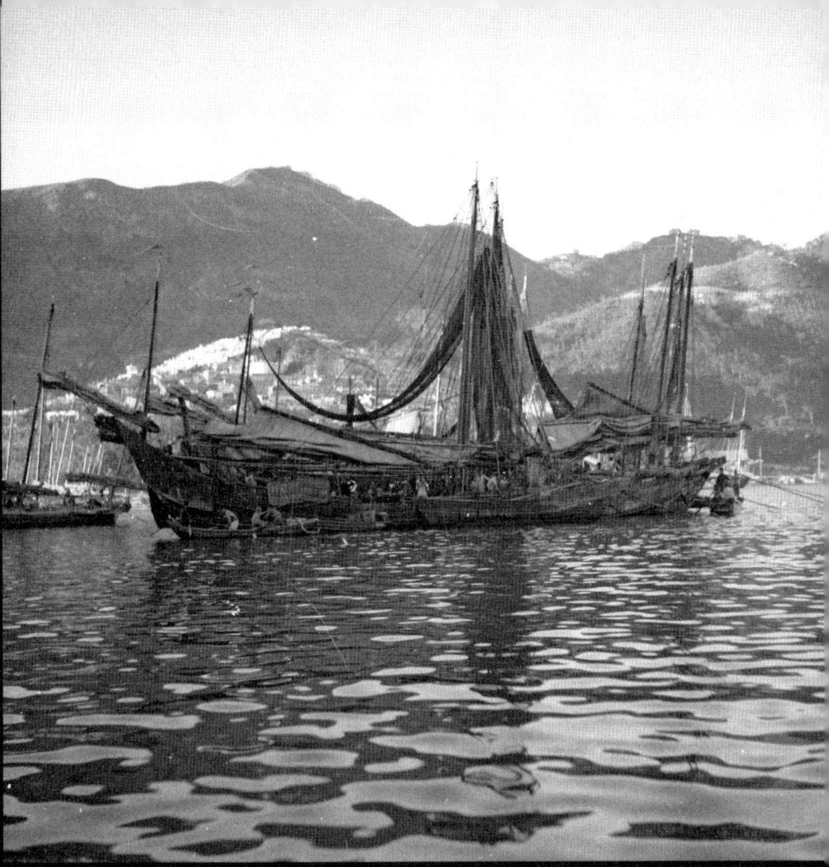
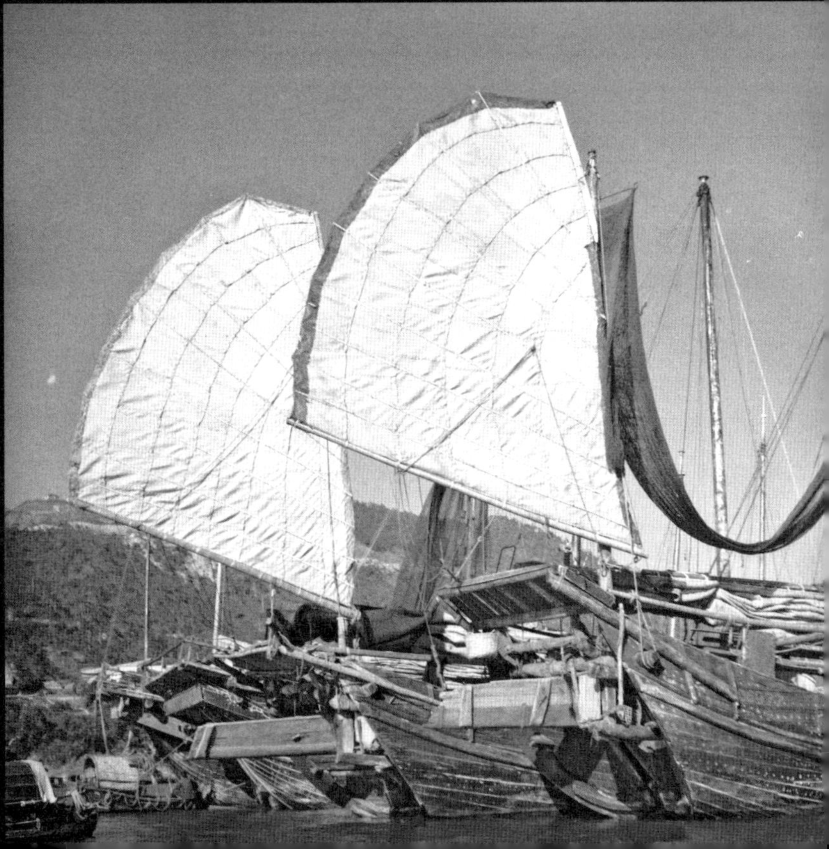

吐露港-5 | Tolo Harbour-5

吐露港-6 | Tolo Harbour-6

吐露港-7 | Tolo Harbour-7

吐露港-8 | Tolo Harbour-8

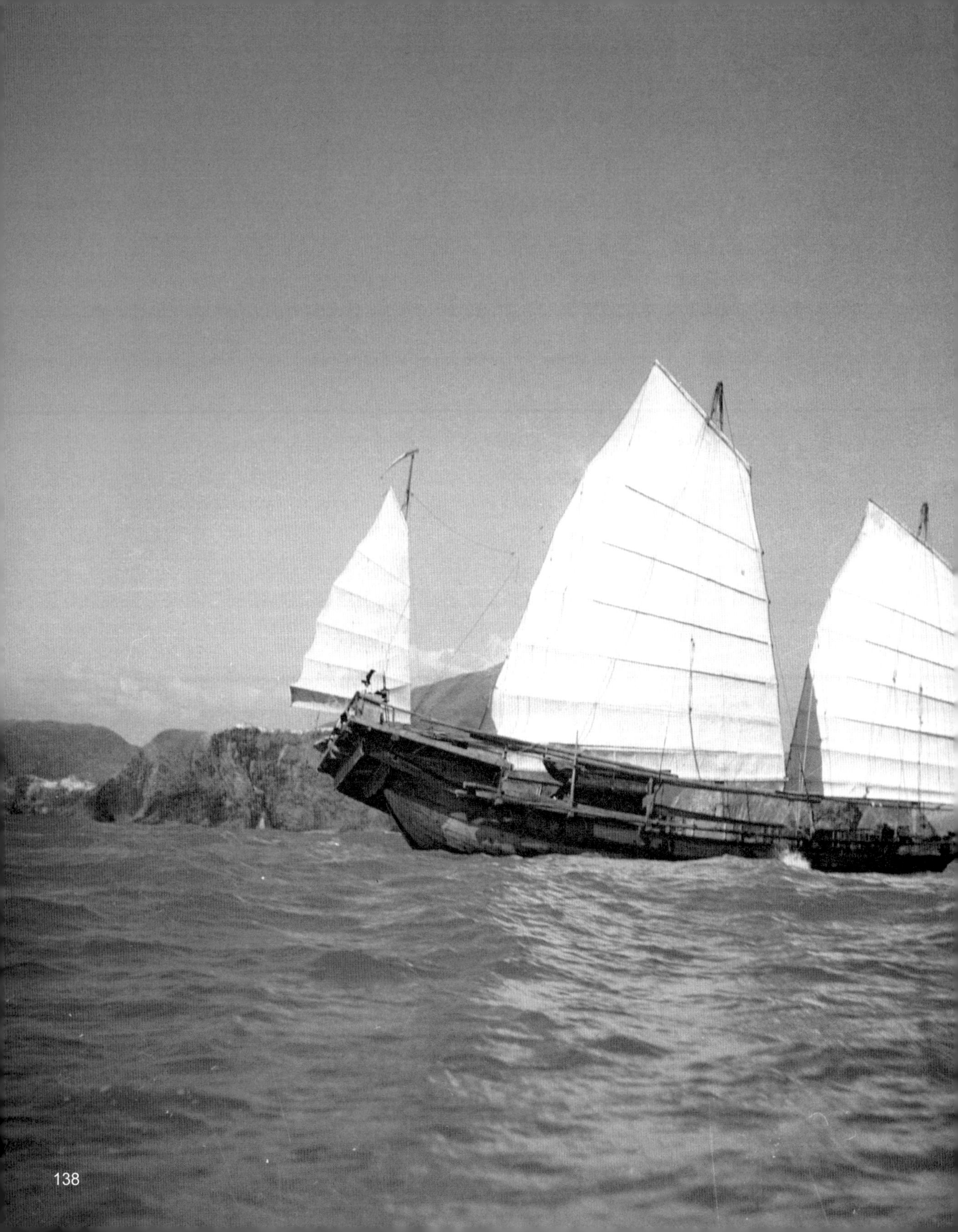

九龙湾渔船

九龙湾渔船通常作业于汕头至海南之间的海域。应同香港渔船一样同属拖网船，一般成对作业。船体特点是：船体分成大小不等的水密隔舱，船艏尖削，船艏到船舯比较平直，然而从船舯至船艉，弧线曲度变大；采用升降开孔舵，可调节深浅高低，船员和舵工在船艉向外伸出的约 2 米的平台上操舵使帆；均为 2 桅，桅杆前倾，但在船艉四分之一处常见 1 根艉桅，只有在渔网撒入海里且主帆不用时才支起，船帆的下风缘弧度较大，接近圆形。

Kowloon Bay Fishing Junk

Kowloon Bay fishing junks usually operated in the waters between Shantou and Hainan. Like Hong Kong fishing junks, they could be categorized as trawlers, generally working in pairs. The main features included the traditional hull divided into different-sized compartments, a pointed bow at the cutwater, and a slight sheer from bow to amidships with a steeper sheer from amidships to the stern. They used hoistable fenestrated rudders. The crew and the helmsmen controlled rudder and the sails from a two-metre platform extending from the stern. They usually had two to three masts, including a foremast canted forward, the mainmast slightly forward of amidships. A small mizzenmast was set on the stern and was only employed when the fishing nets were in the water, as a steadying or balancing sail. The leech of the sails had a large roach that almost formed a circular arc.

九龙湾渔船-1 | Kowloon Bay Fishing Junk-1

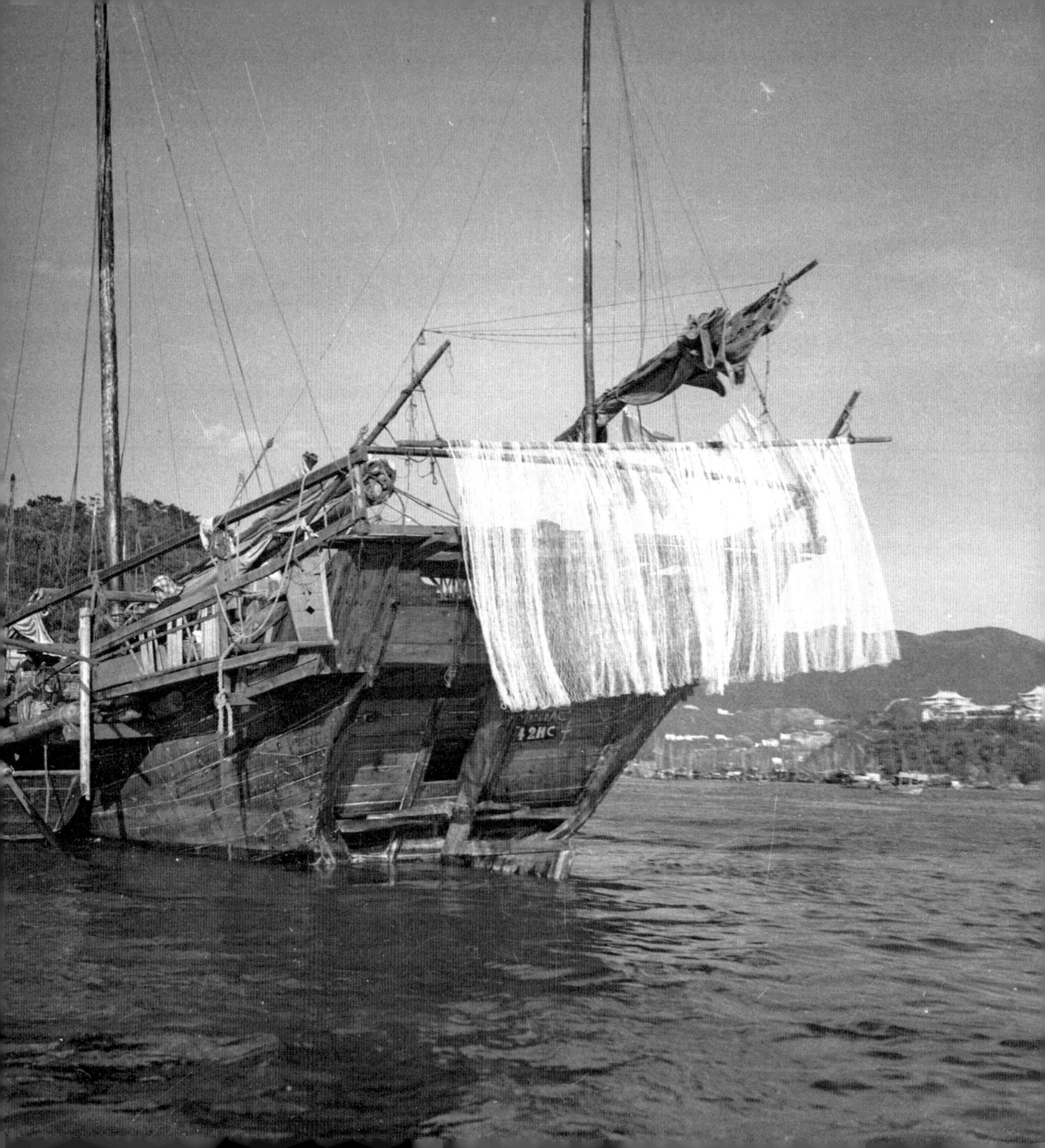
42HC

九龙湾渔船-3 | Kowloon Bay Fishing Junk-3

142

香港渔船

香港渔船又称拖网船,作业于横栏之外的渔场,具有航行性能好、行动敏捷、操纵灵活的特点,适合岛屿暗礁众多的海上作业。香港渔船一般船身无华丽装饰。

Hong Kong Fishing Junk

Hong Kong fishing junks were also known as trawlers. They operated in coastal and offshore fisheries. They had a good sailing performance and their design was readily adaptable to other sorts of fishing and to cargo carrying. Hong Kong fishing junks were not generally highly decorated.

香港渔船 | Hong Kong Fishing Junk

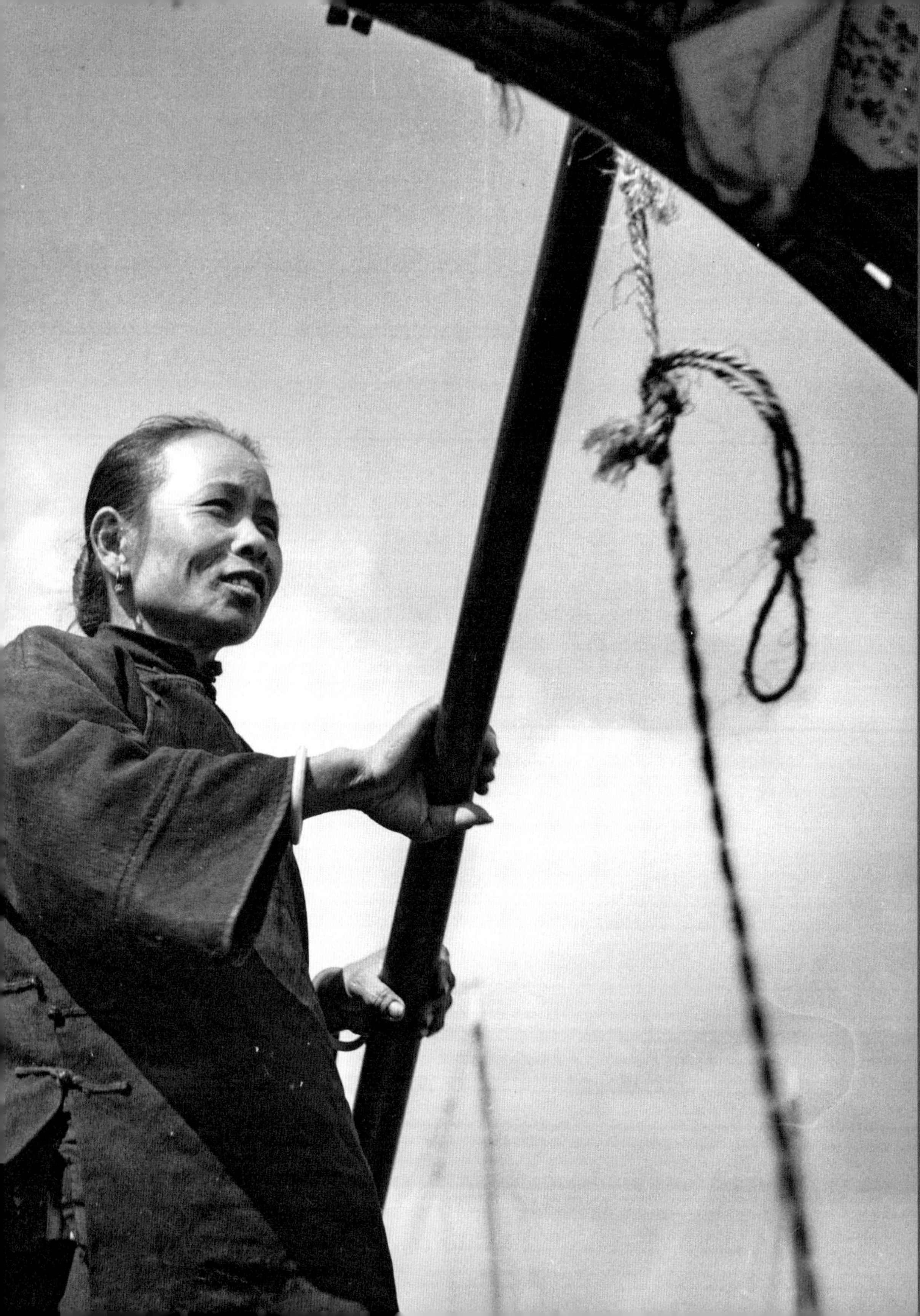

澳 门
Macau

澳门港 | Macau Port

"我们家新订的船下水的时候，妇女是不能上去的，据说那是不洁净，会带来灾难。但是那时我儿媳正好有喜，说是可以'旺船'，仪式办的可热闹了。"

——澳门渔民

"During the launching ceremony, we women are not allowed to be on board. It was said to be unclean, and will bring disaster. But my daughter-in-law had just announced that she was pregnant, which was great news for our family, and prosperous for the newly built junk, so the ceremony is more than lively."

—Fisherwoman from Macau

澳门港

澳门港主要由澳门半岛东侧的外港和西侧的内港组成，位于珠江口西南，其东隔海是香港，西与珠江湾相望，北与珠海相连，南有氹仔。港内风平浪静、面阔水深，适宜帆船停泊。历史上曾是中国与葡萄牙、荷兰、日本、东南亚、美洲等地贸易的重要转口港。明代中叶以后，葡萄牙人以澳门为基地，开展对外贸易活动。清代，澳门基本沿用明代对外贸易的传统航线。鸦片战争以后，随着香港、广州等通商口岸的开放，澳门的对外贸易逐渐走向衰落。

Macau Port

Macau Port mainly comprises the outer port of the east side of the Macau Peninsula and the inner port of the west side. It is located in the southwest of the Zhujiang River estuary, with Hong Kong in the east across the sea, Zhujiang River Bay in the west, Zhuhai Sea in the north and Taipa in the south. The harbor provides an excellent junk haven with a wide harbour and calm and deep waters, which are beneficial for boats at anchor. It was an important intermediary port for trade between China and Portugal, Netherland, Japan, South-East Asia, and American countries. After the middle of the Ming Dynasty, the Portuguese granted Macau as a base for foreign trade. During the Qing Dynasty, Macau was still basically using the traditional route for foreign trade of the Ming Dynasty. After the Opium War, with the opening of other treaty ports like Hong Kong, Guangzhou, Macau experienced a gradual decline in its foreign trade.

天祐昌

罗刹船

罗刹船，又称老闸船，1843年由葡萄人建造用来镇压海盗，最初航行于广州三角洲的澳门水域，多次转手后顺着海岸线进入上海、宁波等地及沿江口岸。因其适宜长江航运，太平天国时期曾被用来走私军火等非法运输。罗刹船均建造于澳门内港，通常采用柚木和樟木，结合了广船和葡萄牙造船技术，船体平底，吃水很浅，通常立3桅，悬挂斜桁帆，船艉和舵遵循广船制式，适宜逆风航行。船体为西式设计，采用前后不弯曲的龙骨，船头有用于支索帆的斜杠，具有葡萄牙造船特点。罗刹船另一特色是船身漆土红，艉楼和艏楼被涂上杏黄色，突出的甲板室被涂成白色，因此中国人又称之为"白蟹壳"。

Lorcha Junk

Lorcha junk, also known as Laozha Chuan, were thought to date from the 1843, when the Portuguese made efforts to suppress piracy in the waters of Macau. However they were also used on the China coast in Shanghai, Ningbo and other ports. Due to their larger cargo capacity and ease of handling, they were used for illegal transport purposes like arms smuggling during the Taiping Heavenly Kingdom Rebellion. Lorcha junks were built in Macau's inner harbour, often made of teak wood and camphor wood. The design combined the shipbuilding techniques from both Guangdong and Portugal. The typical hull had a moderate deadrise and a moderate draft, the rig was usually 3-masted in the traditional junk form with balanced, fully battened lug sails. The stern and rudder sometimes followed the pattern of Guangdong junks, while the bow was always more typical of western vessels. Lorcha junks with a more western hull form sometimes had bowsprits from which fore-and-aft jib sails were hoisted. The result was a vessel with a more weatherly performance than traditional junks, though its capacity to work to windward was often exaggerated. Additional feature of lorcha junks was a red hull, apricot-coloured poop and forecastle, and a white protruding deckhouse, which was called "white crab shell" by Chinese people.

罗刹船-1 | Lorcha Junk-1

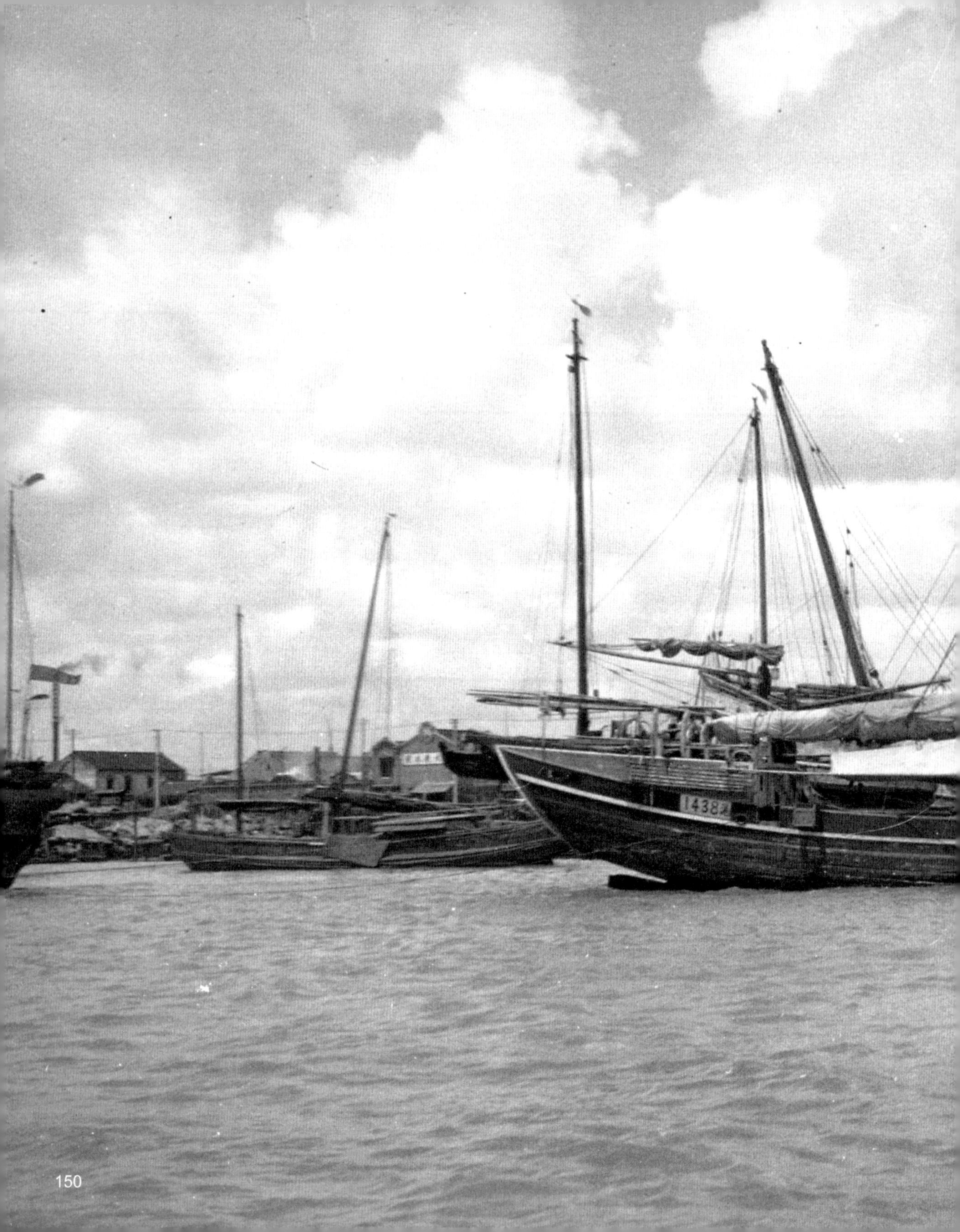
1438

罗刹船-2 | Lorcha Junk-2

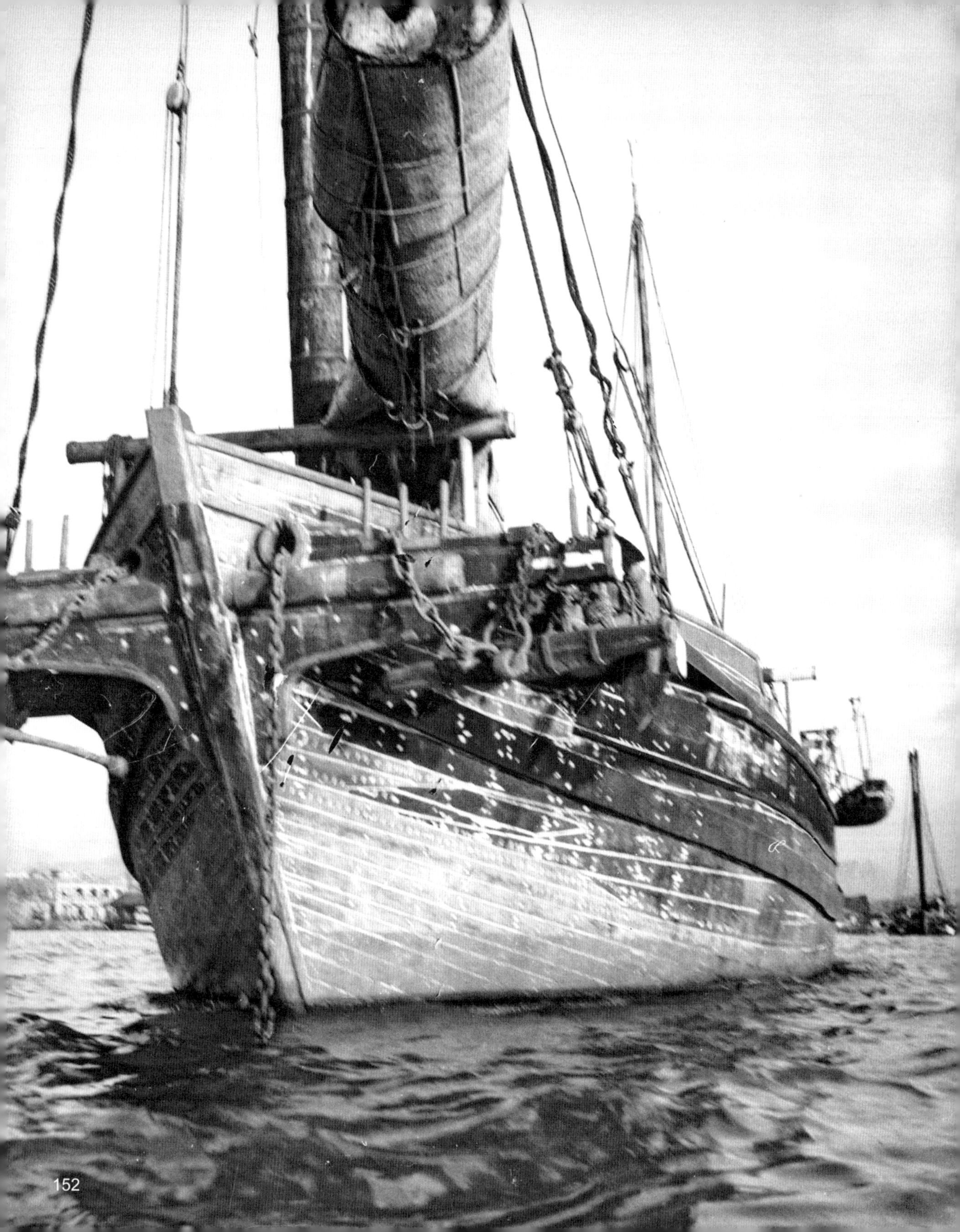

澳门渔船

澳门渔船种类不一,根据捕鱼方式不同,可分为大尾艇、大拖、虾艇、撑罾等。如拖船一般成对配合作业,将渔网系于两船,用铅条压住网口沉入海底。澳门渔船皆传承广船的制式,主要特征是:船体上阔下窄,船艉部开阔,还建有假艄,渔民称为柴肋,用来饲养家禽,大尾艇也因此得名;船艉有开艉型和密艉型,因渔民的住所在此,因此一般建得高大;因要配合渔网等工具的使用,船舷两边会建造搭架等辅助结构;船艏柱与龙骨交接的夹角外贴一件有菱形开孔的木件,类似开孔舵的原理,渔民称为"头夹"。

Macau Fishing Junk

Macau fishing junks could be divided into different types of boats depending on the fishing methods employed. For example, tugboats often operated in pairs so that the net could be tied in between them, pressed by lead bars and sunk into seawater. Macau fishing junks bored the standard form of Guangdong junks, and their main features included: a hull with a wide top and narrow bottom, and an open stern with a false poop used to feed poultry, called "Chai Lei" by fishermen. This feature was also the origin of the name "big tail boats". It had two types of stern, open and closed, the taller style of which was also used as the residence of fishermen and thus was generally built tall. Frames and other auxiliary structures were added to both sideboards to fix nets. Outside the intersection where the bow column and the keel jointed together, a piece of wood with diamond-shaped holes was posted, in a similar principle to a fenestrated rudder, and was used to keep the junk sailing in a straight line and avoid yaw. Fishermen called this a "Tou Jia".

澳门渔船-1 | Macau Fishing Junk-1

澳门渔船-2~4 | Macau Fishing Junk-2~4

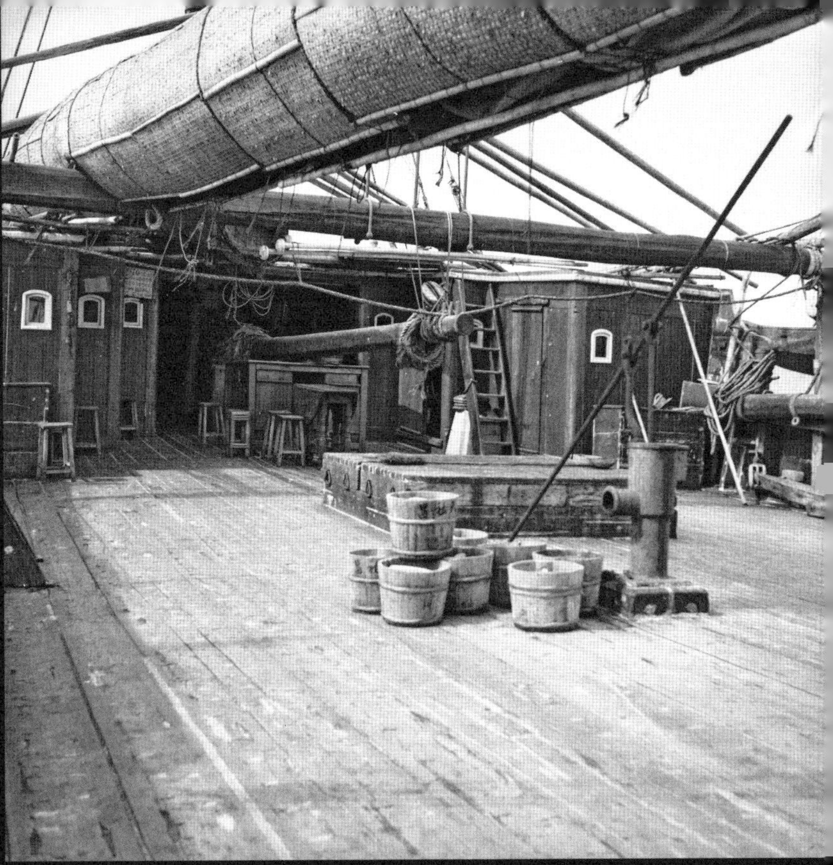

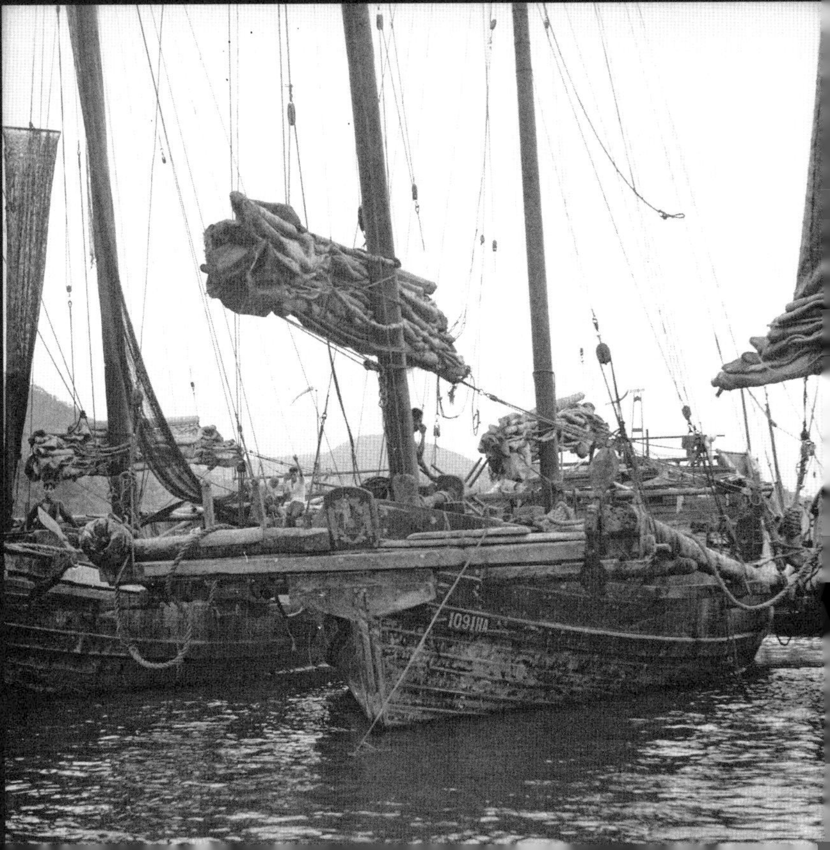

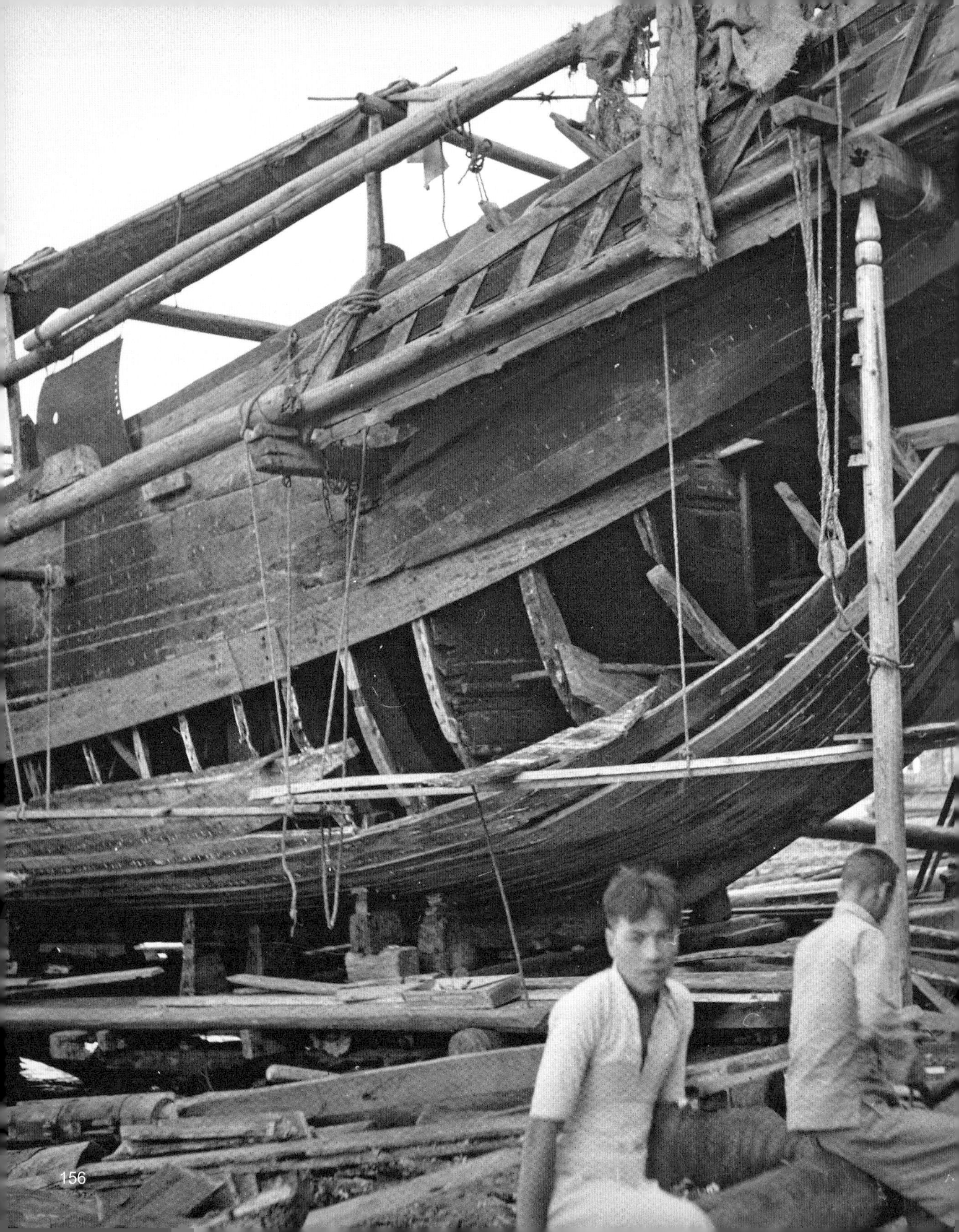

水密隔舱

横向水密隔舱系统是中国木帆船区别于其他地区传统船舶的基本特征。其是指船舱用木板隔开,并在隔板板缝及与船舷的结合处用艌料加以捻缝密封。据清《金门志》记载,除了横向水密隔舱,船体隔舱板之间还会加装纵向隔舱板,称为"蜂房"。考古出土表明,水密隔舱技术在唐代就已出现,宋元时期得到广泛使用。在使用功能上,渔船可用来作为鱼获的存储舱;货船可分舱载货,调整重量和重心的分布,防止船体摇晃时货物移动;商船可作为货主租用面积的租金核算依据。水密船舱结构有两个显著优点,一是如果一舱受到损坏,其他舱不致受累被毁,在保全船只和货物的同时,又便于修复,二是隔舱板横向支撑船舷板,增强了船体抵抗侧向水压的能力。

Watertight Bulkhead

Watertight bulkheads were a basic feature that distinguished Chinese junks from other traditional vessels. Several compartments, usually an uneven number, were created by wooden bulkheads running from bow to stern at irregular spacings. The boards were nailed and clamped together, with the joints sealed by tung oil and lime. Records from the Qing Dynasty "Jinmen Zhi" text indicated that, in addition to the transverse watertight compartments, in some types of junk longitudinal bulkheads named "Feng Fang" were also added. Archaeological records also showed that the bulkhead form had emerged by the Tang Dynasty and thereafter became the basis of Chinese building technique in the Song and Yuan Dynasties. The adaptability of the internal subdivisions allowed their use for different purposes including wet fish storage, separating loads of cargo into different holds or adjusting the distribution of weight and barycentre to prevent the movement of cargo. The bulkhead could also serve as spaces for lettable areas. The use of plugs in the limber holes allowed the containing of flooding resulting from the hull being holed, and also prevented water damage to cargo in unaffected spaces. The transverse bulkhead build system acted, as with frames and deck beams in frame-first construction, as the main transverse strengthener for the hull.

水密隔舱 | Watertight Bulkhead

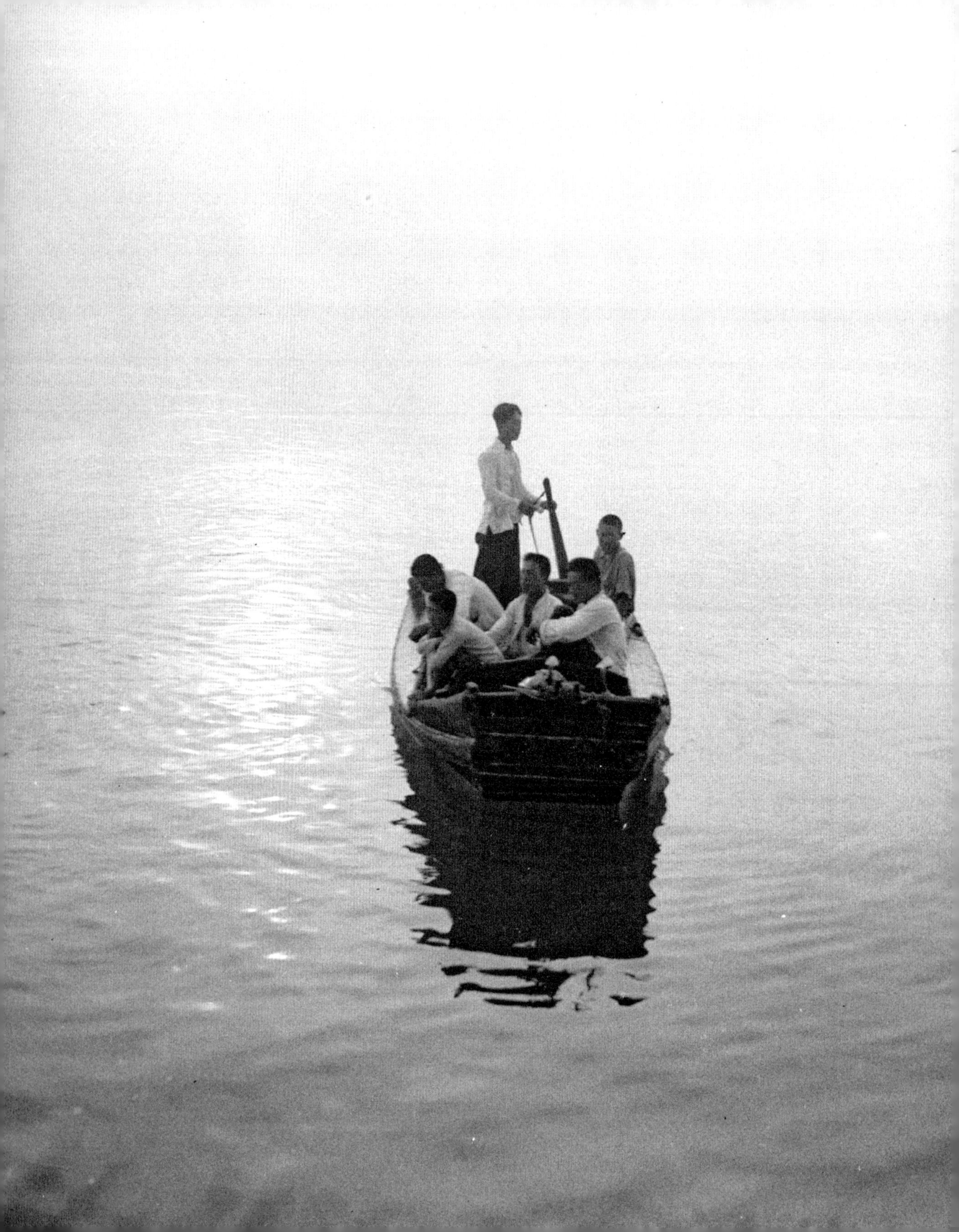

东南亚所见中国船
Chinese ships seen in South-East Asia

越南北圻 | Tonkin Vietnam
新加坡港 | Singapore Port

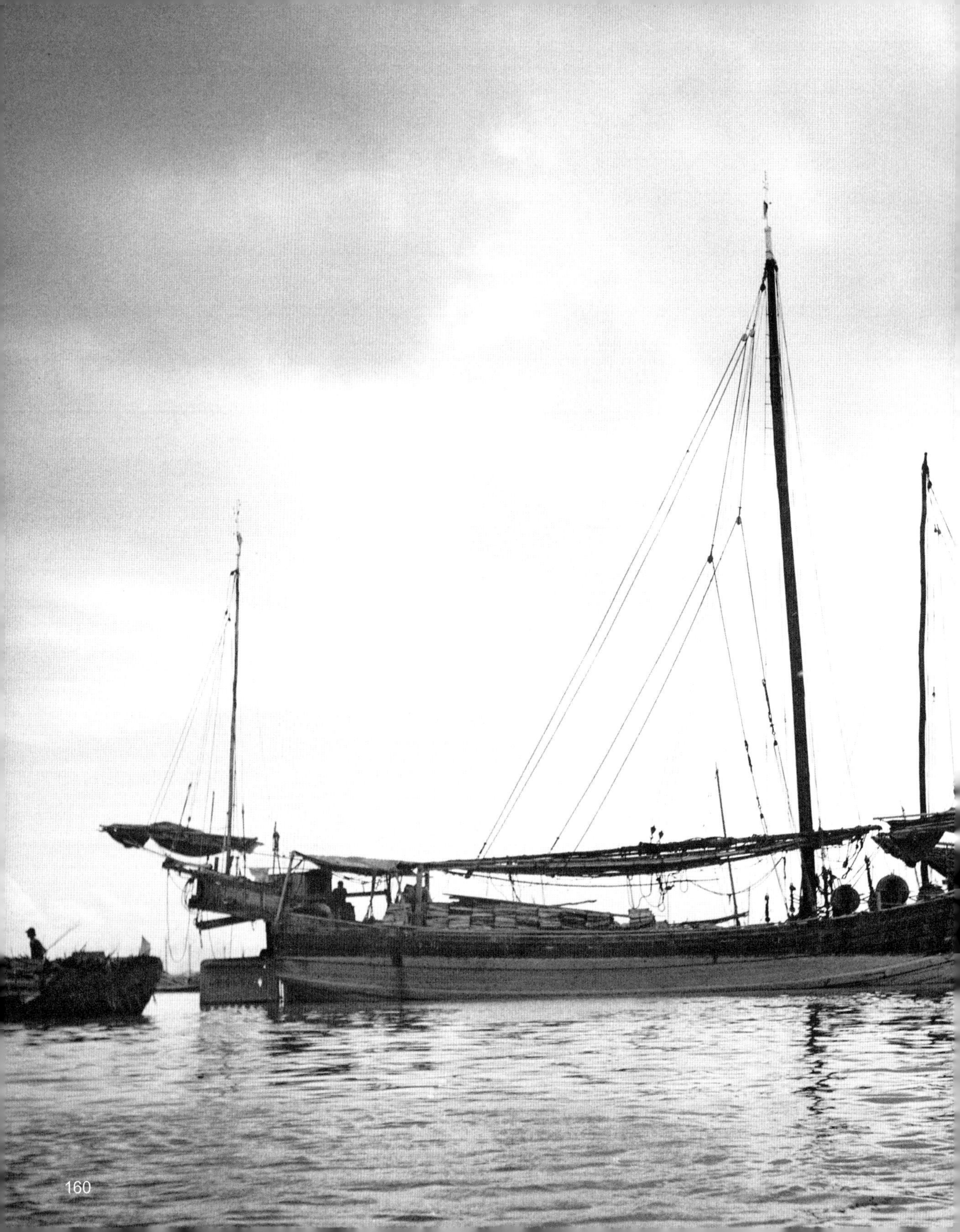

越南北圻

北圻,指旧时越南北部十六省,意为"北部国土",是法属印度支那人口最多的地区,北圻海防是仅次于南圻西贡的第二大贸易口岸,越南北方的进出口货物均由此出入。其出口贸易以原料为大宗,主要是稻米、玉米、橡胶、煤炭等,出口货物中稻米主要输往中国内地,其次是新加坡、法国和印度等地,玉米则全部销往法国,进口贸易则主要从法国进口食品、机械、纺织品等制造品和及半制造品。20世纪30年代前期受世界经济危机影响进口贸易超过出口,后期出口贸易逐渐恢复。

Tonkin Vietnam

Tonkin, the French pronunciation of its Vietnamese name Dong Kinh, was the northern region of modern Vietnam with the largest population of French Indo-Chinese. Its main port is Haiphong, a gateway for northern Vietnam's import and export goods. By the end of the 19th century it was the second largest trading port after Saigon (also known as Cholon) in southern Vietnam, known in French colonial days as Nam Ky, or Cochinchina. Raw materials accounted for a dominant share of the export trade, including rice, corn, rubber and coal. The rice was mainly exported to mainland China, followed by Singapore, Hong Kong, France, India and other places, while corn was wholly sold to France. Imports were mainly food, machinery, textiles, other manufactured goods and semi-manufactured goods from France. In the early 1930s, its imports exceeded its exports due to the world economic crisis, before the gradual recovery of the export trade in the late 1930s.

越南北圻 | Tonkin, Vietnam

新加坡港

新加坡港位于新加坡共和国南部沿海，西临马六甲海峡的东南侧，南临新加坡海峡的北侧，扼居太平洋及印度洋之间的航运要道，是亚太地区最大的转口港，也是世界最大的集装箱港口之一。自 13 世纪开始，新加坡港便是国际贸易转口港。20 世纪 30 年代，尽管新加坡还是英属殖民港口，但此时新加坡与英国的贸易占其贸易总量的比重不大，与美国、中国、日本、澳大利亚等国的贸易量增多。

Singapore Port

Singapore Port is located on the southern coast of the Republic of Singapore, west of the south-eastern Malacca Strait, and south of the northern Singapore Strait. It is the largest entrepot in shipping lanes between the Pacific and Indian Ocean in the Asia-Pacific region, as well as one of the world's largest container ports. Since the 13th century, Singapore was the entrepot of international trade. In the 1930s, despite the fact that Singapore was a British colonial port, its trade with Britain only accounted for a tiny fraction of the whole system, while trade with the United States, China, Japan and Australia increased.

新加坡港-1 | Singapore Port-1

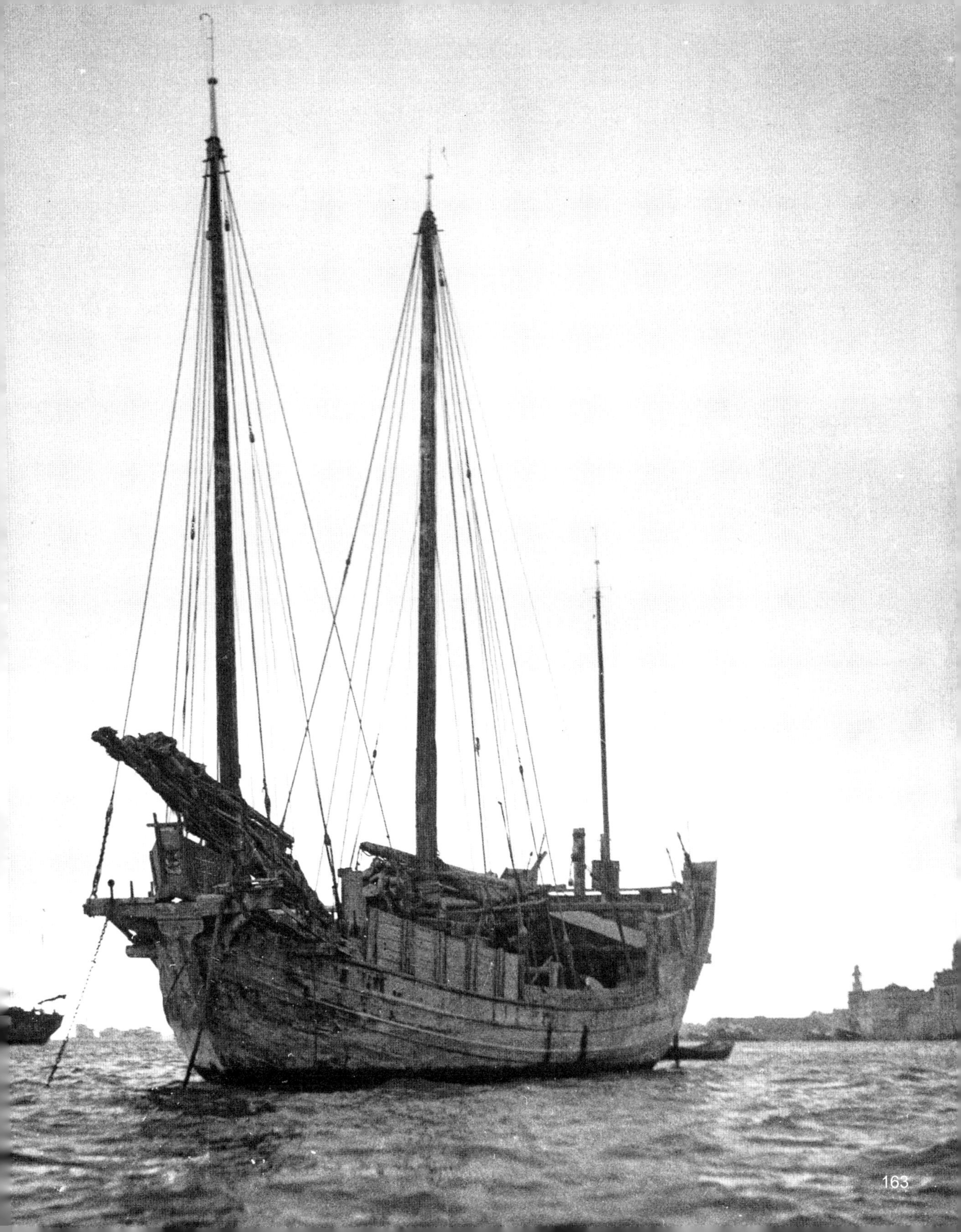

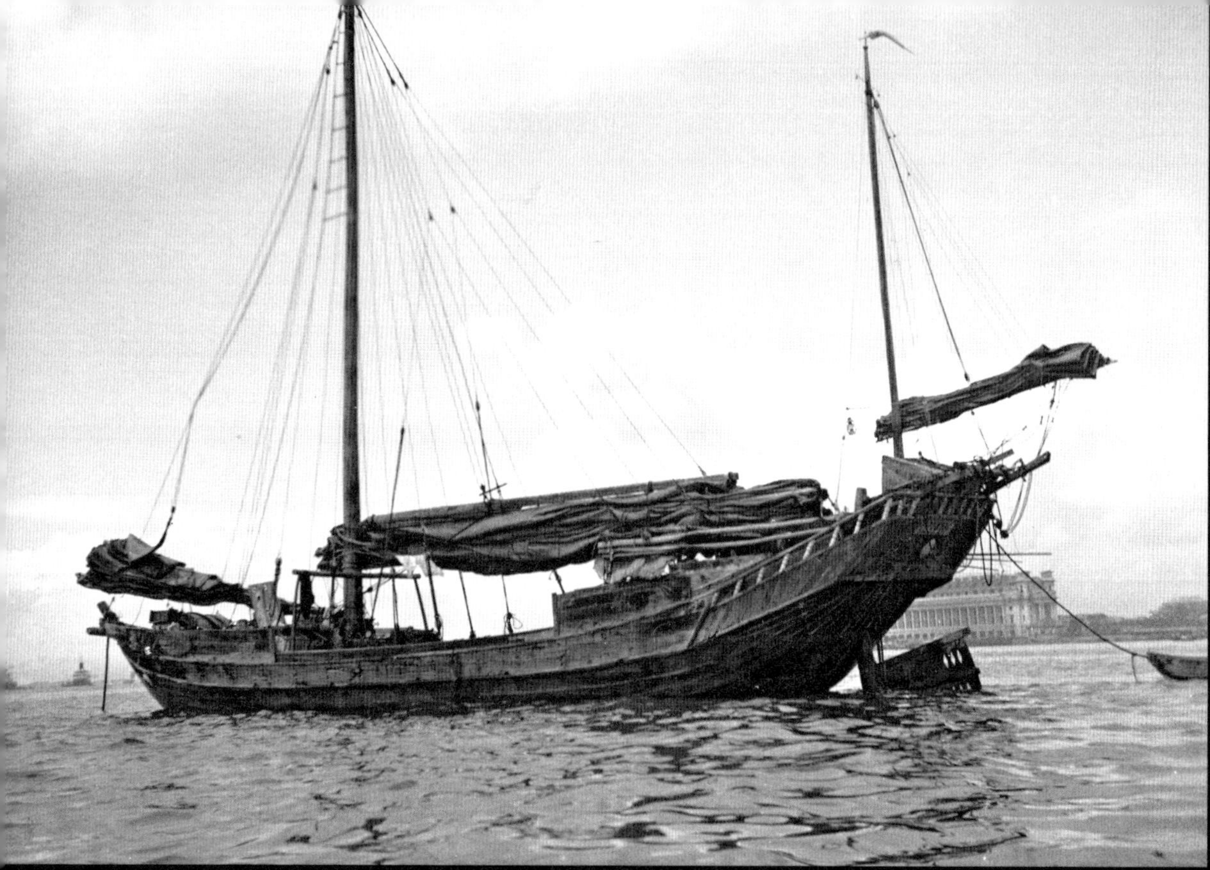

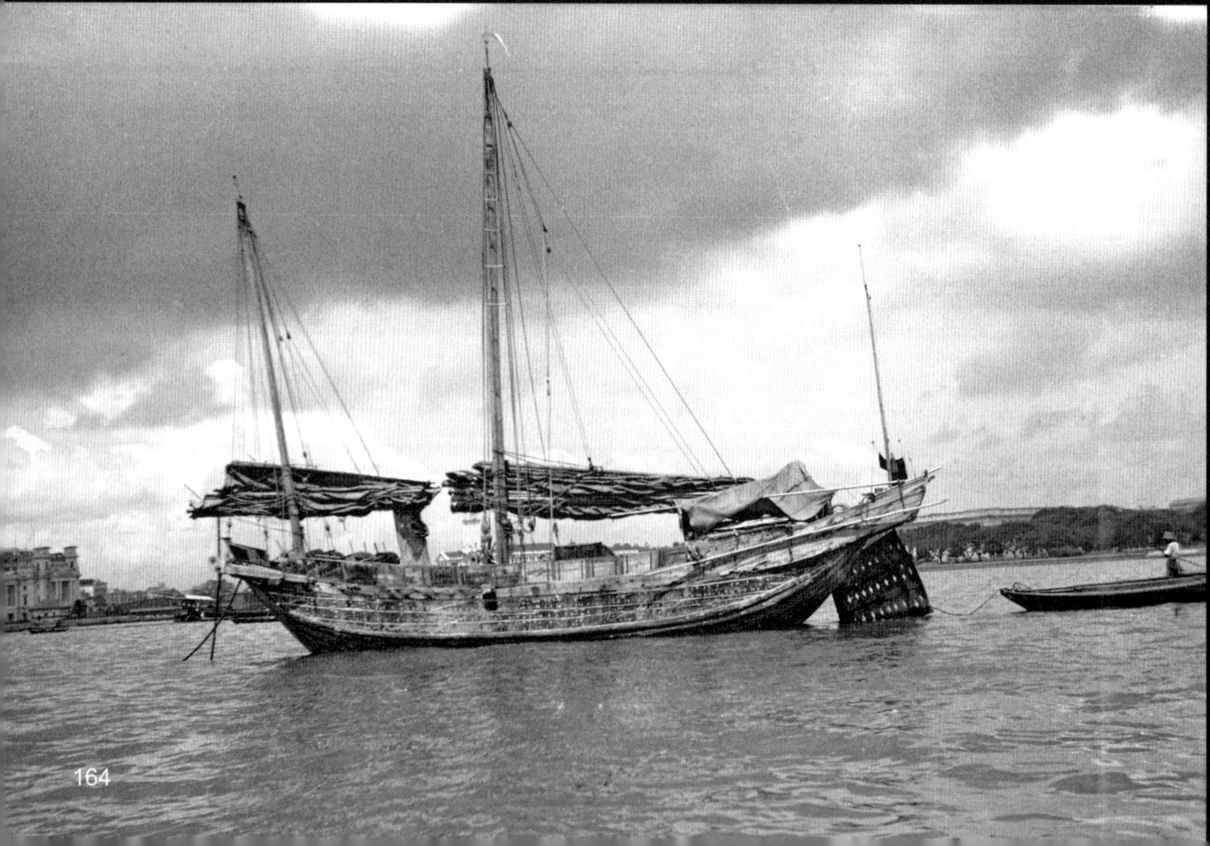

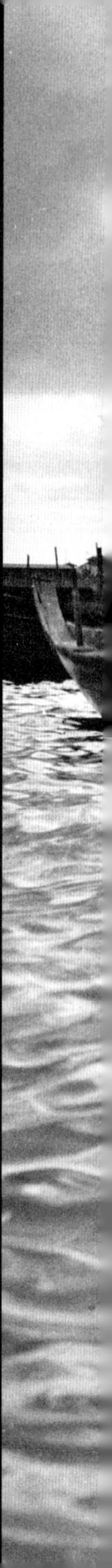

新加坡港-2-4 | Singapore Port-2-4

新加坡港-5~7 | Singapore Port-5~7

167

参考文献
References

曲永义、杜庆余：《山东海洋贸易与海洋文化研究》，山东人民出版社，2014年。

白克敏主编：《航海辞典》，知识出版社，1989年。

王展意主编：《当代中国的水运事业》，当代中国出版社，1989年。

[日] 佚名绘，大庭修著，朱家骏译：《唐船图考证》；[美] V.A.索高罗夫著，陈经华译，陈延杭、王锋校：《中国船》；[美] I.A.唐涅利著，陈经华译，陈延杭、王锋校：《中国木帆船》，海洋出版社，2013年。

丁抒明：《烟台港史（古、近代）部分》，人民交通出版社，1988年。

寿杨宾：《青岛海港史（近代部分）》，人民交通出版社，1986年。

辛元欧：《上海沙船》，上海书店出版社，2004年。

上海社会科学院经济研究所编：《上海对外贸易（1840~1949）》上，上海社会科学院出版社，1989年。

中国航海学会：《中国航海史（古代航海史）》，人民交通出版社，1988年。

樊百川：《中国轮船航运业的兴起》，中国社会科学出版社，2007年。

席龙飞：《中国造船通史》，海洋出版社，2013年。

宁波市对外贸易经济合作委员会编：《宁波市对外经济贸易志638~1995》，宁波出版社，1997年。

周厚才：《温州港史》，人民交通出版社，1990年。

托马斯·霍庇、张敏：《"鲨绫"、"牵缯"与"绿眉毛"——闽浙传统帆船形态及其重建》，《南方文物》2012年第3期。

沈毅敏：《杭州湾商船浅析》，载《跨湖桥文化学术国际研讨会论文集》，文物出版社，2014年。

袁晓春：《8000年的漆与船》，《中国生漆》2013年第4期。

廖大珂：《福建海外交通史》，福建人民出版社，2002年。

席龙飞：《宋元时期泉州的造船与航海》，"泉州港与海上丝绸之路"国际学术研讨会会议论文，2002年。

庄为玑、庄景辉：《泉州宋船结构的历史分析》，《厦门大学学报（哲学社会科学版）》

1977 年第 4 期。

李玉昆：《妈祖信仰在北方港的传播》，《海交史研究》1994 年第 2 期。

徐德志等：《广东对外经济贸易史》，广东人民出版社，1994 年。

蒋祖缘主编：《广东航运史（近代部分）》，人民交通出版社，1989 年。

张晓辉：《民国前期的粤港航运业》，《广东史志》1994 年第 3 期。

黄国信：《区与界：清代湘粤赣界邻地区食盐专卖研究》，生活·读书·新知三联书店，2006 年。

宋应星著，潘吉星译注：《天工开物译注》，上海古籍出版社，1993 年。

明清广东省社会经济研究会：《十四世纪以来广东社会经济的发展》，广东高等教育出版社，1992 年。

崔策：《广东沿海木帆船初探》，《广东科技》2015 年第 14 期。

张晓辉：《香港与近代中国对外贸易》，中国华侨出版社，2000 年。

陈乔之：《港澳大百科全书》，花城出版社，1993 年。

金行德：《广东船研究》，广东旅游出版社，2012 年。

李约瑟著，陈立夫主译：《中国之科学与文明·航海工艺》，台湾商务印书馆，1980 年

邓开颂、黄启臣：《澳门港史资料汇编（1553~1986）》，广东人民出版社，1991 年。

黄洁娴：《澳门木船建造——广东传统造船工艺之承传》，载《航海：文明之迹》，上海古籍出版社，2011 年。

王冠倬：《中国古船》，海洋出版社，1991 年。

聂德宁：《近现代中国与东南亚经贸关系史研究》，厦门大学出版社，2001 年。

WONG LINKEN, *Singapore: Its Growth as an Entrepot Port, 1819~1941*.

From Regional Entrepôt to Malayan Port: Penang' Trade and Trading Communities, 1890~1940, Penang and Its Region: The Story of an Asian Entrepôt.

Basil Greenhill, *Ask to Zumbra: A Dictionary of the World' Watercraft*, the Mariners' Museum, 2000.

后　记

20 世纪 30 年代,一名西方古船爱好者——英国人大卫·威利·沃特斯(David Willie Waters)(后入职英国国家海事博物馆,担任过副馆长)在中国及东南亚沿海港口拍摄了大量纪实照片,真实记录了当时的传统舟船、造船工艺及海港风情等。近年来,这些珍藏于英国国家海事博物馆的历史照片,逐渐引起中英两国社会各界的热切关注。

基于共同的古船情结与研究热情,经过与英国方面卓有成效的坦诚沟通,我们有幸获得了英国皇家格林威治博物馆对这批珍贵照片的出版授权。为了尽早向业界和社会公布这批备受关注的珍贵照片,经过系统整理与初步研究,我们专门挑选了其中 130 余幅照片,并编辑成册出版,名之曰《舢板女孩的微笑》,精彩再现了 20 世纪 30 年代停靠在海港的中国传统舟船的风姿倩影,以飨读者。

《舢板女孩的微笑》一书由国家文物局水下文化遗产保护中心、宝德中国古船研究所整体策划,尤泽峰、姜波负责资料整理、执笔编著及全文统稿。感谢国家文物局水下文化遗产保护中心副主任宋建忠研究员的关心与帮助;感谢英国皇家格林威治博物馆馆长凯文·菲斯特博士(Dr Kevin Fewster)欣然同意在百忙之中为本书撰写序言;感谢藏品与公共事务总监迈克·萨纳先生(Mike Sarna);中国造船工程学会船史委员会副会长、蓬莱登州博物馆馆长袁晓春副研究员,中国船级社武汉规范研究所教授级高工何国卫先生,宝德中国古船研究所袁雁悦博士、林歆女士、常方舟女士和黄艳女士在资料整理过程提出了宝贵意见;香港大学史蒂文·戴维斯博士(Dr Stephen Davis)和皇家格林威治博物馆凯特女士(Miss Kate Mason)、宁波市文物考古研究所周眕恒女士在英文翻译方面给予了无私帮助;特别感谢英国大使馆文化教育处中英文化连线基金的支持帮助;上海古籍出版社编辑吴长青、贾利民、宋佳更是不辞劳苦,为本书的出版付出了辛勤劳动;特此感谢林国聪老师的指导与帮助。值此书稿付梓之际,谨向上述单位和个人致以衷心的谢意。

由于编者水平有限,本书编著过程中出现的疏漏与错误在所难免,尚祈各位读者见谅并指正。

编者

2017 年 5 月

Postscript

In the 1930s, a British Navy officer, David Willie Waters, who was later employed as deputy curator of the National Maritime Museum in the United Kingdom, he took a large number of documentary photographs in China's coastal ports with his camera in his hands, genuinely recording traditional vessels, shipbuilding technology, and harbour scenery at that time. Those historical photographs collected in the museum were no doubt become extremely valuable for research under the theme of Maritime Silk Road. They have gradually raised awareness of this topic among all walks of life in both China and the UK.

Based on shared interests and research enthusiasm, after efficient communication and hard working, we were honoured to be authorized by the Royal Museums Greenwich in the United Kingdom to publish these priceless photographs. Through systematic reorganizing and initial study, we chose more than 130 photos specifically to compile and publish as an album, with the title *Sampan Girl Smiles*, brilliantly reflecting the images of China's traditional vessels in the sea ports of the1930s for all readers.

Sampan Girl Smiles was overall planned by National Centre of Underwater Cultural Heritage of State Administration of Culturl Heritage and Institute of Ancient Chinese Ships, organized,written,compiled and edited by Mr. Zefeng YOU and Dr. Bo JIANG. Our gratitude goes to vice Director and researcher at National Centre of Underwater Cultural Heritage, Mr. Jianzhong SONG's concern and assistance. Our sincere thanks go to Dr. Kevin Fewster, Director of the Royal Museums Greenwich in the United Kingdom, who gladly agreed to write a preface despite his busy schedule,and Mr. Mike Sarna, Director of Collections and Public Engagement at museum. We also appreciate valuable ideas and suggestions during the compilation of the book from Mr. Xiaochun YUAN, vice present of the Ship History Committee of China's Marine Engineering Society and the Director of Dengzhou Museum in Penglai; Professor Guowei HE from Standardization Institute of China Classification Society in Wuhan; Dr. Yanyue YUAN, Ms. Xin LIN, Ms. Fangzhou CHANG and Ms. Yan HUANG of the Institute of Ancient Chinese Ships. We need to thank Dr. Stephen Davis from the

University of Hong Kong ,Miss Kate Mason from the Royal Museums Greenwich and Ms. Yiheng ZHOU from Cultural Relic Archaeological Institute in Ningbo for their selfless help in English proofreading. Our deep gratitude goes to the support of the British Embassy Culture and Education Office Chinese and English Cultural Links Fund.Our deep gratitude goes to Mr. Changqing WU,Mr. Limin JIA and Ms. Jia SONG, editors of Shanghai Classics Publishing House and others' timeless hard work for publishing this book on time. Special thanks to Mr. Guocong LIN. On the occasion of its publication, we need to express out sincere gratitude to the organizations and the persons mentioned above.

Due to the limitations of our editorial abilities, oversights and mistakes were inevitable in the process of compilation. We hope all readers will excuse us and kindly point them out so that they can be corrected.

Editors
May, 2017

图书在版编目(CIP)数据

舢板女孩的微笑/国家文物局水下文化遗产保护中心,宝德中国古船研究所编;尤泽峰,姜波编著.—上海:上海古籍出版社,2018.4
ISBN 978-7-5325-8490-1

Ⅰ.①舢… Ⅱ.①国… ②宝… ③尤… ④姜… Ⅲ.①航海-史料-中国-近代 Ⅳ.①U675-092

中国版本图书馆CIP数据核字(2017)第143057号

照片版权来自英国皇家格林威治博物馆 伦敦 2018年

出版合作:皇家格林威治博物馆(包括国家海事博物馆、凯蒂萨克号、皇家天文馆以及女皇屋)

Photographs © National Maritime Museum, Greenwich, London, 2018
Published in association with Royal Museums Greenwich, the group name for the National Maritime Museum, Cutty Sark, the Royal Observatory, and the Queen's House. www.rmg.co.uk

舢板女孩的微笑

国家文物局水下文化遗产保护中心
宝德中国古船研究所 编
尤泽峰 姜波 编著

上海古籍出版社出版发行

(上海瑞金二路272号 邮政编码200020)

(1)网址:www.guji.com.cn
(2)E-mail:gujil@guji.com.cn
(3)易文网网址:www.ewen.co

上海丽佳制版印刷有限公司印刷

开本787×1092 1/16 印张11.75 插页4 字数100,000
2018年4月第1版 2018年4月第1次印刷
ISBN 978-7-5325-8490-1

J·581 定价:118.00元

如有质量问题,请与承印公司联系